A New
Political Economy

COMPASS PROGRAMME FOR RENEWAL

A New
Political Economy

COMPASS PROGRAMME FOR RENEWAL

Edited by
Hetan Shah
and Martin McIvor

in association with
Lawrence & Wishart

London 2006

Lawrence and Wishart Limited
99a Wallis Road
London
E9 5LN
www.lwbooks.co.uk

Compass
Southbank House
Black Prince Road
London SE1 7SJ
www.compassonline.org.uk

First published 2006

British Library Cataloguing in Publication Data.
A catalogue record for this book is available from the British Library

ISBN 1 905007 50 7

Members of the New Political Economy Working Group

Kate Bellamy	Neal Lawson
Robin Blackburn	Roger Levett
David Clark	Hywel Lloyd
Sarah-Jayne Clifton	Toby Lloyd
Colin Crouch	Martin McIvor (chair)
Jon Cruddas	Ross McKibbin
Will Davies	Mary Mellor
Pat Devine	Frances O'Grady
David Donald	Guy Palmer
Larry Elliott	David Purdy
Alan Finlayson	Howard Reed
Ian Gough	Guy Rubin
John Grieve Smith	Jonathan Rutherford
Sue Himmelweit	Hetan Shah
Alan Hutton	Robert Taylor
George Irvin	John Taylor
Joe Irvin	Paul Thompson
Nick Isles	Andrea Westall
Hilary Land	Stuart White

All contributions were made in a personal capacity. This book aims to reflect the mix of ideas and balance of discussion that emerged, but it should not be taken to be representing the views of any particular member of the working group and individual contributors do not necessarily agree with every conclusion in the book.

About the editors
Hetan Shah is policy director at Compass. He was previously director of the New Economics programme at the new economics foundation, a think tank.

Martin McIvor is a policy researcher with academic interests in political philosophy. He was Director of the left think-tank Catalyst from 2002 to 2005.

Acknowledgements

In addition to the members of the working group, we would also like to thank for valuable input and comments: Ash Amin, David Anderson, Jessica Bawden, Simon Bullock, David Coats, Emma Dawnay, John Earls, Paul Ekins, Alex Evans, Andrew Glyn, Romilly Greenhill, Stephen Haseler, David Held, John Hills, Martin Hyde, Helen Jackson, Roger Jeary, Tom Jenkins, Bill Kerry, Brendan Martin, Iain McLean, Mick McAteer, Mahua Nandi, John Newton, Jeremy Nicholls, Tim Page, Philip Pearson, Lee Roberts, Meg Russell, Paul Skidmore, Gavin Smart, Robert Wade.

Particular thanks to Sally Davison at Lawrence and Wishart for managing the production and publication of the book.

Thanks to the Joseph Rowntree Reform Trust for providing general funding to Compass. Thanks also to the Barry Amiel and Norman Melburn Trust, Unison, and the following Compass members for providing financial support for the Programme for Renewal: Rebecca Allen, Jack Andrews, Keith Barnard, Victoria Barr, Barbara Barrett, Tony Belton, Clara Bentham, Roy Bentham, Paul Blomfield, Jeffrey Boss, Philip Bradley, John Bull, Joseph Buttle, Margaret Camina, Philip Carter, Peter Cawley, Sarah-Jayne Clifton, Julian Coman, Jeremy Cooper, Paul Cornick, John Crisford, Mike Cuddy, Hugh Davies, Marilyn Evers, Geoff Garrett, Dan Godfrey, Alan Goodfellow, Miranda Grell, John Grieve Smith, Megan Griffith, Ian Hancock, Ryan Heath, David Higgins, Ron Hikel, Del Hosain, Norman Hunt, Alan Hutton, Martin Ignatius Gaughan, George Irvin, Martin John Holst, Philip Jones, Graham Kemp, Peter Kenyon, Maurice Line, Ruth Lister, Margaret Maden, Linda McAvan, Des McConaghy, Peter McGinty, Fiona Millar, Denis Mongon, Andrew Morton, Lawrie Nerva, Neil Nerva, Ray Newton, Wendy Nicholls, Jim Northcott, Richard Pennell, Denis Pethebridge, Anne Rafferty, Howard Reed, Fraser Rennie, Judith Roberts, Tim Roberts, John Robertson, Tony Robinson, Meg Russell, Jonathan Rutherford, Roger Sainsbury, Chris Sewell, Henneke Sharif, Eric Shaw, Victoria Silver, Peter Smith, Nigel Stanley, Jean Stead, Steve Strong, Kathy Sutton, Lindsay Thomas, Alan Tomlinson, Glyn Tudor, Bob Tutton, Giovanni Vitulli, Laurence Whitehead, Larry Whitty, David Williams, Barbara Williams, Robin Woodburn, Richard Young.

Contents

The Compass Programme for Renewal

Compass is a pressure group providing direction to people and organisations who want a more democratic and equal society.

The historic project for social justice and democracy has stalled and is in urgent need of renewal. After the failings of post-war socialism, the rise of Thatcherism in Britain and the domination of neo-liberal values and practices across much of the world, the response of New Labour has been mixed.

New Labour was a creation of pessimistic times. Now, over a dozen years since its birth, its legacy could be described as good in parts. Yes, it has humanised more elements of a rampant market than the Tories ever would have done, but, paradoxically, it has also deepened the grip of the market on society.

Crucially, New Labour adapted itself to the economic rationalism of the neo-liberal project rather than attempt to go beyond this debilitating hegemony. It has failed to break with the old ways of doing politics, and has not responded to the new threats of the market. The problem with New Labour is that it is neither new enough, nor Labour enough. It is a project that has run out of steam.

Building on the partial successes of New Labour, but also learning from its failures, it is time to think again. The Compass Programme for Renewal is the start of that process. Launched just after the 2005 general election, the programme is an ambitious attempt to rethink ideas and strategies for a more equal and democratic society. In the process it offers a space to build alliances between individuals and organisations who share the goals of Compass, so that they may over time become a reality. It is to the synthesis of ideas and organisation that Compass aspires.

The central objective of this politics is to enable people to become the masters of their own destiny. As Gandhi described, we want to be the change we wish to see in the world. Markets have an important but necessarily restricted role to play: the ability to manage our world can only be achieved by working together as citizens, not as individualised consumers.

For freedom to flourish, we need more than greater equality as individuals, so we can all live fulfilled lives. We also need the institutions and processes that will allow us to act together to manage the world around us. True choice requires the possibility that we might change the terms of choices offered to us – to want, and be able to build, a different kind of world.

There are three interlocking elements to this renewal process:

- A vision of a good society – to fuel our political aspirations
- A new political economy that supports this vision – exploring how we can become more enterprising and creative, but also manage markets for the good of society as a whole, at the same time sustaining the life of the planet

- A revival of democracy and the public realm, so that we have the capability to withstand the pressures of an over-encroaching market, and to act collaboratively to determine both what the good society is, and how to progress towards it.

A New Political Economy is the second in a series of three short books that form the first stage of the Programme for Renewal. They are a collaborative product of many people's time, experience and knowledge. This collaboration includes not just the input of the members of the Working Groups listed in each book, but also submissions from Compass members, findings from desk research, expert interviews, and commissioned 'thinkpieces' that can be seen on the Compass website.

The analysis offered in the books is challenging, and mirrors the threats and opportunities society faces. The policy strategies are not yet systematically formed but are strongly symbolic of a fresh, popular and achievable new politics.

The strategic challenge we face is in linking reforms that are achievable now with a process that transforms our society. The aim is not just a marginally better world, but a different one, where the values of democracy, equality and solidarity, and therefore true freedom, become the new hegemony. Power and principle are two sides of the same coin. How do we balance them effectively?

We don't have all the answers, but these three books mark the start of an overdue debate. We actively welcome contributions and criticisms, in writing or via the space for debate on our website. Compass is also taking the debate out to the countries and regions of Britain with a Renewal Roadshow. Our aim is to engage with progressive organisations and individuals the length and breadth of Britain, including MPs, council leaders, charities, social entrepreneurs, progressive businesses, environmentalists, trade unions, community leaders and think tanks. And after this we aim to conduct a similar process at the European level, in order to build international networks that make a more equal and democratic society a reality.

You can contact Compass as follows:
Website: **www.compassonline.org.uk**
Email: **info@compassonline.org.uk**
Postal address: **Southbank House, London SE1 7SJ**
Telephone: **020 7463 0633**

Foreword

There has been little explicit debate about a new political economy for a long time. You have to go back to the Alternative Economic Strategy (AES) of the mid to late 1970s for the last time there was a coherent attempt to define a new political economy. Well for the left at least. And we have paid the price.

On the right the economy is all they have thought about. For them it is always 'the economy stupid', and they have dominated the terms of political debate as a consequence. Neo-liberalism is in essence the supreme example of political economy. It takes a particular vision of the individual as rational economic operator and builds around this conception a set of economic institutions, practices and, most importantly, a culture that supports the view that we are all in essence possessive individuals. For neo-liberals we are machines constantly calculating how best to secure advantage over others to struggle to satisfy selfish preferences and desires. Freedom is the freedom to win or lose in the market place. The upshot is a 'common sense' view that we would rather compete than co-operate, that you 'cannot buck the market', and that wealth creation is based on heroic CEOs and entrepreneurs, who must have the right to manage without interference from the state or their workers. Ultimately it takes you to a view that there is no such thing as society. As Gordon Gekko said in Oliver Stone's *Wall Street*, 'It's all about bucks kid, the rest is just conversation'.

That is what political economy is – the application of a set of political values to economic thinking and action. Neo-liberals cleverly wrap their political economy into a belief system that claims free markets are inevitable and natural – in the USA even God-given. This of course is palpable nonsense. Markets and economic systems are made by us, moulded by our thoughts and shaped by our actions. We set the rules and determine the dominant values base – usually to serve one set of vested interests over another.

Neo-liberalism is the most recent example of a dominant political economy, but let's look at another – the welfare economics of the post-war period. This was a political economy built on a different set of assumptions; it recognised both the creative and destructive power of free markets, and knew that avoiding a repeat of the pre-war depression years would require organised intervention. The likes of Keynes and Beveridge, very different sorts of liberals, had the wit and imagination to construct new forms of global management and welfare supervision. These were institutions for their time and their day, and they created historic levels of growth and equality.

But the post-war settlement ossified. What was right for the mass, centralised and more deferential post-war era was not right for the 1980s and beyond. The collapse of socialism in the East and the loss of confidence of social democrats in the West opened the door to the advance of the neo-liberals, a determined political faction that had been thinking and organising in a coherent fashion for little more than a decade. They swept all before them and we live in their dark shadow today.

New Labour and markets

So where does this leave New Labour? At one level New Labour marked an important breakthrough. It took economics seriously and has proved it can manage economic stability through Bank of England independence and a wider macro-framework. Since 1997, through initiatives such as the New Deal, Britain has had relatively full employment, and measures like tax credits and the minimum wage have at least meant no further increase in the extraordinary gap in wealth and income that Thatcherism bequeathed Britain.

But New Labour has steadfastly refused to change the terms of debate about the essential primacy of the market. It has been described by Stuart Hall as performing 'a double shuffle':[1] it seeks to humanise the market, through initiatives like the minimum wage, but at the same time it deregulates markets, through flexible labour market strategies, and creates new space for markets to commodify what remains of the non-market sphere through the commercialisation of the public sector. It takes one step forward and two back.

New Labour's political economy is not the continuation of Thatcherism – at least not in terms of means. Both Thatcherism and New Labour accept as benign the influence of globalisation, and Tony Blair has said that 'complaining about globalisation is as pointless as trying to turn back the tide'.[2] But Thatcherism made it clear it was up to the individual to thrive – all government should do is get the state off their back. New Labour, on the other hand, while placing equal stress on the role of the individual, actively uses the state to help employability in a global economy, through supply-side measures such as education and training. New Labour is much more humane than Thatcherism, but it still accepts the ultimate authority of the market.

In this New Labour inverts the historic principle of social democracy – it makes the individual, and through it society, the servant rather than the master of the market. So the economy becomes largely untouchable. Globalised economic competition means that intervention is always inefficient, as it stops markets from being free; and in any case, if we erect barriers to the freedom of markets, transnational companies will simply shut up shop and go to where regulation is lightest. We face the eternal blackmail of companies like HSBC, who regularly threaten to shift their HQ abroad, in a race to the bottom, of who can deregulate faster and further.

But the surrender to market forces has further profound and ultimately devastating implications for any realistic centre-left agenda. The primacy of the market as the creator of all wealth and value becomes pervasive. New Labour holds that it is through the market that we create our welfare policy, as the best welfare is a job. So everything is directed at employability, and all must be sacrificed in the name of economic efficiency. This is the core of the New Labour political economy – that economic efficiency and social justice go hand in hand.

Economic efficiency and social justice can go together – just look at Sweden, Finland, Denmark and Norway. But not always. Economic efficiency is taken by some to mean paying the lowest wages at the lowest employment standards. This may be economically efficient in the most narrow cost/benefit sense (though this is arguable), but it is certainly not socially just. This view of efficiency leads down the low road to international competitiveness, which becomes inevitable once politicians cede control over the economy.

And this is just the start of the problem. Once we kneel before the market, everything is sacrificed in its name. The public sector is commercialised to open up new markets, communities are ripped apart as jobs disappear, national identities are distorted as institutions like the BBC and the Post Office cannot stand the competitive heat, community cohesion becomes more difficult, and of course the environment is destroyed. In terms of the alleviation of poverty we are left running up the down-escalator, as pay increases at the top warp any sense of social inclusion, and tax increases for redistribution fall permanently from the political agenda. Feelings of insecurity and anxiety are now rife across all social groups, because of pensions that won't cover our old age, the outsourcing of even white-collar jobs, and the perpetual slog of working all hours to keep up with a consumer culture that determines our status in society. The ultimate transformation is of people, who are conditioned to fend only for themselves and to believe that there is no solidarity between us. We become what the neo-liberals said we are – just lone individuals looking after number one. The road to serfdom is now paved by the market.

New Labour cannot triangulate away the tensions between labour and capital. You don't have to believe that there is some class war going on to know that there are inevitable tensions between the interests of labour and capital, between society and the market, and that the relationship between capitalism and democracy can be zero-sum. Labour market flexibility and an assault on poverty cannot go hand in hand – we have to choose what is most important to us.

Ultimately the price exacted by the neo-liberal hegemony is political. If politicians only exist to serve the interests of the free market then what is the point of swapping one set of managers for another? That's not my view, but the message from millions who no longer bother to vote. It is also the message from the ranks of former Labour Party members who have left – now outnumbering those who remain. We may be reaching a point of no return, where our ability to control the economy through democratic forces has so withered that the prospects of ever being able to manage capitalism again can feel very bleak. Has Mrs Thatcher won – is there no alterative?

Reasserting society

Our saving grace is both the laws of physics, that state that to every action there is a reaction, and the very nature of capitalism itself. Capitalism is a machine programmed to do one thing – make profit. This is its great strength. There is no morality, no sentiment, just a never-ending quest to increase profits, locally, nationally and ultimately globally. This ruthless focus is what makes capitalism so dynamic and creative. But its strength is also its weakness. Enough is never enough. Capitalism always ends up eating itself. It's like a shark that has its stomach cut open and briefly feeds on itself. The notion that everything can be reduced to market economics ends up leading to the destruction of the social conditions in which markets actually thrive. Just as welfare economics came to the rescue of a discredited capitalism over sixty years ago, so society must now reassert itself in its on-going battle for supremacy with the market. If the war and the depression were the impetus in 1945, it is now primarily the environment that must be saved by a new Keynes and Beveridge.

To achieve this we need to build a common sense for a new political economy. This must be based on the idea that it's not a question of whether we intervene to stop the excesses of market freedom, but of when. At the moment neo-liberalism forbids intervention to regulate markets, it is only allowed to clear up the mess at the end – whether that is the scars of social division, crime or environmental damage. This is hugely wasteful. We need to make the case for early strategic intervention to stop the chaos markets inevitably create. The case for regulation can be made popular. Just as the brakes on a car allow the vehicle to go faster, so the right regulations can encourage the right types of growth. We need to be bolder, too, in pointing out where and when markets fail. Just look at the energy market in the UK and the huge price rises. We need a respect agenda for corporations that are out of control, and ASBOs for destructive capital flows that wreck our communities. We need to match the work ethic with a care ethic. And finally we need to rewrite the myths of history and the post-war 'failures' that weren't such failures after all. As this book shows, growth in the era of managed capitalism far outstripped growth in the neo-liberal era.

Ultimately our project is simple. It is to return to an agenda that makes society the master of the market. This book charts the course. It is based on a fundamentally different belief about what constitutes human nature from that of the neo-liberals. We believe that people are co-operative, altruistic, solidaristic and caring. We are wonderfully complex and deep. We want to create, play, love, invent and dream. We are curious, not just profit-maximising. We don't want to learn just to earn, but desire emotional satisfaction, social reassurance and acceptance.

We need to build economic and social institutions, processes and platforms that reflect this richness of the human spirit. We believe the best in people, and that true freedom to manage our own lives is ultimately an issue of equality and solidarity – it has nothing to do with the inequality and division of the market.

The failure of society to master the market in the past was essentially due to the failure of the old state. In both its revolutionary and reformist guises the state was a creature of its centralising times. Ross McKibbin says that New Labour is 'best understood as Thatcherism tempered by Old Labour'.[3] We must reject both Thatcherite neo-liberalism and the old statism of the past if we are to forge a new political economy. That is why the third part of this Programme for Renewal trilogy is about the democratisation of the state into a responsive, adaptive and inclusive entity that can enter into continual negotiation with the market, to hold it in check, boost its performance and save it from itself. The democratic left welcomes globalisation and the more open society it creates. But our goal is to make people, not just to make profits. This demands double democratisation – of nation states and global institutions.

Mrs Thatcher and the neo-liberals made the world in their image. Chillingly she said that 'economics is the method, the objective is to change the soul'.[4] Not enough has changed since her time, because we have failed to develop a different notion of a political economy. There is always room for manoeuvre – ways to shape our destiny if we want to. That demands a view of the good society we set out in the first publication in this series. But change comes only when people struggle for what they believe to be right.

Neal Lawson
Chair, Compass

Executive summary

What kind of economy do we need to create the good society? Britain has experienced strong economic growth and stability over the last decade. But we are relying on mass indebtedness to keep the economy afloat, from individual consumer debt right the way to the ballooning US deficit. Capitalism is increasingly commodifying, invading the public realm and marketising public services. It is creating higher levels of inequality, unprecedented levels of systemic risk and major environmental problems. The UK is locked into a 'low road' to success, based on low levels of investment and poor skills. Present policy focuses upon deregulating capitalism and then picking up the pieces afterwards. This is a vastly inefficient way of doing things. Instead the economy needs to be designed to promote quality of life, social justice and environmental sustainability as primary goals. Building on the proposals in *The Good Society* to promote equality, this book puts forward a series of policy proposals to help manage capitalism and put the UK economy onto a 'high road' to prosperity.

At the individual level this includes:

- Better employment protection through a living wage and better working conditions

- More access to training and skills, including a legal right to time off for training for unskilled workers

- Better paid parental leave

- More support for caring responsibilities through a better care workforce

- A work life balance and ability to both work and care for others through a maximum 48 hour working week and an extension of the right to request flexible working to all

- Measures to promote green homes not just on new build but also on existing homes which constitute 99 per cent of housing

- Access to 'smart tariffs' for energy which give access to low price energy up to a certain basic level (dealing with fuel poverty) but then charging higher rates for extra consumption

At the corporate level this includes:

- A focus on quality of working life including giving employees greater control over their workplace

- Greater duties for corporations to take all stakeholders (rather than just shareholders) into account when making decisions

- Higher levels of company transparency, especially when operating in the public realm, such as when taking part in PFI schemes
- Recognition of the needs of all corporate actors such as small businesses, the voluntary sector and social enterprises rather than a pure focus on the needs of big business
- Greater shareholder activism and legal action to prevent boardroom failures receiving fat cat salaries

At the market level this includes:

- Greater use of smart regulation to promote innovation and to build quality markets that work in the public interest
- Universal service obligations to protect the weakest – e.g. to provide ATMS in poor areas
- Greater environmental regulation to help make the socially conscious choice an easy choice for consumers – e.g. to not put stand by switches on electronic items
- Better competition policy to prevent large scale monopolies
- Measures to reduce investor short-termism
- The use of public sector procurement to achieve social and environmental aims

At the UK level this includes:

- Raising taxation levels over time towards Scandinavian levels to fund better public services and mitigate the inequality caused by globalisation
- Reform of the fiscal framework to switch the overall tax burden from hitting the poorest hardest to being progressive, and to move towards greater environmental taxation including carbon taxes.
- An annual tax on wealth to deal with the UK's shocking inequality of life chances
- Industrial policy measures including support for environmental industries through a decentralised energy system using Combined Heat and Power stations, renewables and clean coal, to make sure the UK has a share in this world market
- Rebalancing economic activity from the South East to other regions, and in turn easing pressures on the housing market
- A national Standing Commission on the Quality of Working Life
- Better transport infrastructure aimed at giving job seekers greater

mobility, and at making cities more environmentally sustainable through congestion charging

- A land value tax to reduce housing market booms and busts, and to help fund infrastructure such as low carbon transport
- New measures of well-being, social justice and environmental sustainability to help promote good quality economic activity

At the European level this includes:

- Greater commitment to working at the European level to shape globalisation
- More expansionary European economic policies including a European Recovery Fund
- Strengthened European social and environmental regulations
- A new funding stream to achieve the Millennium Development goals, such as a levy on international air travel
- Reform of foreign aid to get rid of so called 'phantom aid' which does not benefit recipients

At the global level this includes:

- Allowing poorer countries to follow their own economic policies rather than being forced to follow neo-liberal orthodoxy through IMF and World Bank strictures
- Using trade sanctions against countries that do not participate in international agreements about climate change
- Rolling back intellectual property laws to promote greater innovation
- Enabling countries to introduce capital controls both as a revenue raising measure and to protect their economies against instability
- A new global reserves system and international clearing union on the basis of Keynes's proposals over sixty years ago
- Making multinational codes of conduct more enforceable, and introducing transparency to their lobbying activities
- A global cap on carbon emissions and a global carbon trading scheme
- Measures to reduce global oil dependence

These measures would help to create a managed capitalism that will outperform the present deregulated system that we have, leading to prosperity, quality of life and a more equal, sustainable society.

1 The good economy

We seek equitable development which ensures all groups in society, not just those at the top, enjoy the fruits of development; we seek sustainable development which includes preserving natural resources and maintaining a healthy environment; and we seek democratic development in which citizens participate in making the decisions that affect their lives, and countries and communities have ownership of the policies.

In the years to come we must build anew our understanding of the relationship between democracy, equality, environmental protection and growth. In other words, we need to move beyond the Washington consensus of the 1980s, a creature of its times which narrowed our growth and employment objectives. Which assumed by liberalising, deregulating, privatising and getting prices right, private markets would allocate resources efficiently for growth. This has proved inadequate for the insecurities and challenges of globalisation.[5]

Chancellor Gordon Brown MP

We can only judge if we are going in the right direction if we have an idea of where we are trying to get to. What is the economy for? Too often the economy (narrowly defined) is wrongly assumed to be an end in itself. The good economy should advance the good life and help us to create a good society. It is not merely a means to pay for these things – a good economy should itself embody and actualise our values of social justice, quality of life, mutual responsibilities, democratic accountability and environmental sustainability.

The good economy provides for public goods as well as private consumption. Generating tax revenues to pay for excellent public services is a leading purpose and benefit of prosperity, not a drag to be minimised and apologised for.

The good economy promotes social justice. Inequality and poverty are redressed through progressive taxation to fund redistributive benefits and services, which are universal and free at the point of use unless there are compelling reasons otherwise. Women, minorities and disadvantaged groups are treated equally and people are fairly treated in the marketplace.

The good economy is a caring economy. It provides living wages, secure pensions and affordable housing for all. It supports a progressive shortening of working hours, with productivity gains taken as time as well as income, as happened through much of the twentieth century but has stalled since the 1980s. It offers everyone the opportunity to enjoy the fulfilments of both work and caring, rather than having too much of one or the other. It supports the household, care and voluntary economies.

The good economy is a democratised and accountable economy. It promotes good working conditions, democratic workplaces, more work time flexibility and more employee control over work. It contains responsible corporations held to account through legal and fiduciary duties and frameworks. It has a more collectivist framework for decisions, not a purely market choice driven approach. It is embedded in a social Europe and international governance mechanisms, and helps promote sustainability, pro-poor development and democracy worldwide.

The good economy is environmentally sustainable. Tax and pricing structures make conserving energy and resources profitable, and waste costly. Smart regulation prevents damage before it happens, rather than trying to clean it up afterwards, and creates opportunities for green businesses.

The good economy outperforms the deregulated 'feral' economy in traditional economic terms. By preventing businesses from causing social and environmental damage, it removes the need for expensive remedial programmes, allowing better use of public resources while still improving the public realm. Public interest decisions improve the long-term viability of businesses and their resilience to trade and environmental shocks. Contented and secure workers bring more to their work, are better able to meet its challenges, and more ready to be innovative and enterprising.

But the good economy measures its success not primarily in terms of monetary growth, commercial competitiveness, or narrow efficiency, but in terms of human well-being, longer-term resilience and security, and environmental sustainability. It is one in which people want to live and work, and where companies invest with confidence.

2 The new capitalism

The UK economy under Labour's management has been improving in many respects and for many people. We have enjoyed consistent stability, steady growth, and rising employment. Success in knowledge intensive industries has brought real prosperity for many people in many areas while the government has developed innovative policies to redistribute income, regulate employment, and regenerate communities, which have benefited the disadvantaged.

But these positive measures have had to contend with background trends and powerful forces in the economy that have frustrated more progressive ambitions. Some of these realities are summarised below so that it is clear what challenges we face in constructing a democratic political economy that can better realise social justice, quality of life and environmental sustainability.

What is the reality of the new capitalism of today? The following are the key interrelated features of the new capitalism that define the context we find ourselves in:

- financialisation, globalisation, and insecurity
- inequality and the 'hourglass' economy
- commodification and consumerism
- resource depletion and climate change
- varieties of capitalism

Financialisation, globalisation and insecurity

Many discussions of political economy today start with 'globalisation' as the basis of intensified competition and industrial restructuring, and associated problems of instability and insecurity. But many of the 'negatives' associated with globalisation are not an inevitable consequence of increasing international interdependency and economic integration, but of the particular forms this has taken following the deregulation of national and international financial markets over the past three decades. This is based on 'neo-liberalism' – a loose grouping of ideas which include an emphasis on markets, very strong property rights, a smaller role for the state, balanced budgets and financial liberalisation. Neo-liberalism is based upon economic theories which presume perfect competition, perfect information and perfect risk markets. But these conditions never exist.

The result has been a new economic climate of 'financialised' capitalism or 'casino capitalism' in which the requirements of contemporary capital markets, dominated by institutional investors, dictate that firms and governments prioritise short-term shareholder value above all other considerations such as consumer needs, workforce development or longer-term corporate and industrial strategy. The annual turnover of foreign exchange has grown from $17.5 trillion in 1979 to more than $300 trillion today. Most money is invested in speculation – only around 5 per cent of investment goes into new share issues. In particular the growth of hedge funds which trade derivatives – extremely complex financial products which are difficult to regulate – increases the systemic risk in the entire financial framework, as was shown in the 1998 Asian crisis which was triggered through the trading activity of a hedge fund.

Companies have become increasingly focused upon financial re-engineering and perpetual restructuring, manifested in successive waves of downsizing and delayering, and more active management of corporate assets through divestment, merger and acquisition as they seek ways of cutting costs and raising revenue to improve financial performance.[6] This is a process that has been driven by politics – the creation of market infrastructures has been driven by rich nation states.

Growth strategies for firms therefore manifest a bias against continuity and employment stability; and other trends, such as greater use of outsourcing and sub-contracting, also lessen the incentives and clear responsibilities for employers to invest in human capital. Whilst a small minority of employees have sufficiently mobile, high value knowledge assets to survive and prosper, more and more employees bear the burden of restructuring and insecurity, low morale, excessive workloads and pressures on pensions and domestic life.[7]

In the UK our seeming prosperity is built on a trade deficit of £6bn a month, and an explosion of private sector and individual debt. We owe more than £1 trillion between us, and unsecured debt makes up around a fifth of this – the average household owes more than £7000 in unsecured debt. We have got used to low inflation and interest rates because Chinese workers have kept the prices of goods low. This is likely to end as oil price rises feed through the economy and inflation is rising, even in China. Insolvency and bankruptcy rates are on an upward trend, and it will not take much to tip our indebted citizens into major difficulties in making their repayments, creating what has been called a 'first world debt crisis'.[8]

At a global level, the relatively favourable growth record of the USA relative to the Eurozone has been facilitated by its large government budget deficit generated under George W. Bush. In 2004, the US budget deficit was nearly 5 per cent of GDP. Because both the US government and the private household sectors spend more than they save, this gap is reflected in a large and growing external trade deficit – over 6 per cent of US GDP in 2005 – a gap that must be financed from abroad. To a significant degree, US expansion has acted as a Keynesian 'motor' of the world economy, particularly in the 1990s when labour productivity was rising and financial markets were buoyant. However, much as with a domestic business cycle, there is growing anxiety today about whether deficit-fuelled growth is sustainable. In short, the 'twin deficit' is potentially a large threat to world financial stability.

Since the US dollar is still the world's main reserve currency, the world's central banks, all of which hold dollar reserves, in effect lend money to the US. So too do countries like Germany, Japan and China which, because they run a trade surplus, can export capital to the US. This lending is helped by the fact that European and Asian households are generally net savers. By definition, a trade deficit in one part of the world must be offset by a surplus somewhere else; over all, the sum of the world's financial flows must balance. Thus, recent US growth has been made possible not just because government and consumers in the US spend more than they earn, keeping demand buoyant, but because EU (and other) governments are prudent and households spend less than they earn. This basic principle is often forgotten in comparing the US and EU growth records. The member states of the EU-15 run a surplus on their current account transactions with the rest of the world, in contrast to the growing US trade deficit. In 2004, Germany overtook the United States in the total value of its exports. Over the past 10 years the EU-15's exports to the rest of the world have increased from 7 to 11 per cent of total GDP; in the US, by contrast, the share of exports in GDP over the same period has stagnated. The faith in the US dollar as the reserve currency is based on its ability to grow. If confidence and hence the exchange rate collapsed and a recession ensued, the US would not be able to service its debt, causing economic disaster not just for the US but globally.

The pillars which provided the security which the post-WW2 generation came to expect – the welfare state, inclusive labour markets and family networks – appear to be crumbling. Part of the insecurity we see is based upon the transfer of risk from the state and employers to individuals. For example in relation to pensions we are expected to use capital markets and the financial services industry to provide for our retirement. But the structures of the financial system are not fit for purpose and do not command the trust of consumers, so people do not make adequate provision. Similar patterns exist in relation to health and social care. We are also seeing major transfers of risk and liability between generations: PFI schemes, failure to reform pension systems, resource depletion and economic growth at the cost of climate change are all examples of shocking intergenerational transfers of risk. Alongside this we have seen the retreat of the state from the provision of core goods and services such as health, social care and pensions. But this is a conscious political choice, not an inexorable result of globalisation.

We are living in a speculative, destructive form of capitalism that is profoundly unhealthy for our global economy and our society, and which benefits only a minority. It has meant a ruthless pursuit of short-term financial performance at the expense of other forms of capital such as human capital – the strategic investment in knowledge and skills; and social capital – the social fabric of trust, commitment and cohesion upon which all economic activity ultimately depends. We have seen individualisation at the expense of the collective and the short term prioritised at the expense of the long term. It has also engendered an environment of insecurity and risk, the burden of which is being systematically shifted onto those in society least able to protect themselves against it.

New Labour's strategy has been to build people's resilience in face of the turbulence. Whilst this is important, it has not been complemented with a regulatory approach that lessens the risks themselves. The kind of economy we are in cries out for new forms of global and local corporate governance that can re-regulate aspects of capital markets, and for measures to enhance the quality of working life and protect employment conditions in the most vulnerable sectors. We need to change future investment flows towards 'good growth'. Regulation could produce greater productivity over all and prevent the race to the bottom (e.g. in the treatment of workers) that results from the unregulated pursuit of individual profit. There is also room for the state to play a full role in the provision of core goods and services such as health and pensions. These are required to help citizens negotiate their way through a more uncertain and insecure world.

Inequality and the 'hourglass' economy

Financialised capitalism has proven to be a grossly unequal capitalism, multiplying the advantages of the privileged and wealthy while frustrating the aspirations of the many for more rewarding forms of economic participation. This is not inevitable. The period after the 1930s until the 1970s has been termed the 'Great Compression' for the way that incomes first came closer together and then grew at the same rate, and the way that taxation on income, capital gains and inheritance became steadily more progressive. In the early 1970s Britain was one of the most equal of the rich nations.

Britain has become home to some highly productive and internationally competitive enterprises, from 'blue chip' conglomerates to small scale 'start-ups', in knowledge-driven-sectors such as chemicals and pharmaceuticals, high-tech engineering and equipment, media and creative industries, and financial services.

These have provided significant numbers of people with productive, empowering, and well-remunerated forms of work. But too much of the new employment created in recent years has been deskilled, insecure, and poorly paid, prompting labour market experts to describe an 'hourglass' economy characterised by a marked polarisation between lovely 'MacJobs' and lousy 'McJobs'.[9]

Over all the UK still invests far less than its competitors in research and development, in workforce skills and training, and in physical capital and infrastructure, and the effects are felt in the quality, intensity and remuneration of millions of working lives. This is a direct result of the deregulated labour market, which reduces the incentives to invest in the labour force except for senior staff. There are concerns about quality of working lives, and some evidence of declining job satisfaction (though this is of course hard to measure).[10] Those bearing the brunt include the women and migrant labourers who provide the cheap and poorly protected labour to our growing service sector, and families and communities in traditional industrial areas who have been hit hard by the continuing loss of jobs in our manufacturing sector. This world can easily seem remote to policy-makers and opinion-formers in central London, but it is the harsh reality for much of the rest of the UK.

The inequalities in pay are grotesque, with the average FTSE chief executive paid 113 times more than the average UK worker. This distorts the entire economy, with city bonuses heating up the London housing market and making it unaffordable for many ordinary people, and interest rates having to rise to cool the top end of the housing market.

The hourglass economy is also manifested in a widening polarisation in the quality of people's working lives, and in increasingly unequal distribution of income and wealth. The Labour government has attempted to counteract these trends through modest re-regulation of the labour market and real redistribution through the tax credits system. There has also been some effort to shift a greater portion of Britain's workforce onto the 'high road' of economic prosperity, through a developing national skills infrastructure, tax relief for research and development, and use of grants and loan guarantees to encourage innovation in strategic areas such as environmental technologies.

But so far these measures have only served to slow, rather than reverse, the trends towards socio-economic polarisation. There has been some flattening of the post-tax income distribution across the bulk of the population, but some disadvantaged groups continue to fall behind, while incomes at the very top continue to soar away from the rest. The concentration of wealth in the hands of a few has been increasing (from a very unequal starting point) since the mid 1990s and we have seen a rise in asset poverty amongst households since the 1980s – a rise in the proportion of households with no savings. Trickle-down economics has patently failed.

As explored in more detail in *The Good Society*, measures of income and wealth give only one indication of the multiple dimensions and far-reaching social consequences of economic inequality. Behind these figures lie widening inequalities of power and participation, security and opportunity, autonomy and well-being, that entrench and perpetuate divisions and exclusions based on gender, ethnicity, disability, and geographical locality. Such disparities are corrosive, undermining social cohesion, and, it is increasingly understood, having a significant impact on health and life expectancy.[11] Social mobility is also seizing up: life chances in the UK are determined greatly by parental income, and this is more the case than a generation ago. Evidence also shows that intergenerational mobility has declined at a time of rising income inequality.

Inequality has been justified by politicians as a necessary route to economic growth and wealth creation, and to pay for merit and risk taken by entrepreneurs. But there is no evidence that prosperity requires inequality, nor that inequality has brought prosperity. Forty per cent of the *Sunday Times* rich list inherited their wealth.[12] It is not the rise of an elite super rich that drives forward the economy; it is the hard work of millions of ordinary people that success depends upon.

Commodification, individualism and consumerism

The Good Society shows that we are living in a social recession, and evidence from 'well-being' surveys shows that the UK is now gaining very little in quality of life terms from increasing aggregate wealth.[13] Why is this? One important factor is that contemporary capitalism tends to invade spaces and commodify experiences which were previously not marketised. This is true – in different ways – of nature, of childhood, of cultures, of public spaces and of public assets. Where it is not investing in productive innovations that can genuinely enhance human well-being, capitalism's relentless drive to self-expansion can all too easily translate into an invasive commodification of activities that are already being performed outside the market economy – in households, communities or the public sector. Much of today's economic 'growth' takes the form of such incorporation – squeezing the spaces in which we find other ways to express ourselves and relate to one another, and ultimately threatening to undermine the social base upon which all economic activity depends.

Capitalism's invasion of personal time is now perhaps the most ruthless process of all. It occurs both through production and consumption. In production the drive for competitiveness forces not only longer working hours but much higher individual productivity within them – leading to greater feelings of pressure and experience of stress. Meanwhile ever-increasing social pressures to consume – including the 'consumption' of leisure activities – leaves less and less time for genuinely non-consumption activities; most of all, for relationships with others based on care and friendship, not exchange. This results in the paradox faced by many employees today who, given the opportunity, would happily sacrifice current consumption levels if they could reduce their working hours and so have more time for their families, friends, communities and hobbies and look after their own health – those things which well-being research suggests are some of the true sources of quality of life.[14]

We are also seeing a pervasive commodification of the public realm, driven by an effort to turn voluntary and public services into sources of private profit, and reflected in a generalised infection of public and social spaces (from politics to education) with commercial and consumerist values. It is argued in *Democracy and the Public Realm* that markets are amoral and allocate value according to economic power and influence not rights or needs, and that people do not want the same level of choice available in the high street carried over into public services. Research shows that imposing choice on people can be counterproductive and that, for example, citizens welcome the idea of collectively run pension schemes as 'everyone pulling together'.[15]

We live in a society dominated by a focus on private choice as a way to the good life. Galbraith coined the phrase 'private affluence, public squalor'. Economies which curtail public goods for private choice lead to public squalor and high levels of inequality. But in an hourglass economy social goods such as public services are crucial for supporting the low skilled workers at the bottom of the hourglass. And there are many things we cannot choose alone: for example a good public transport system or a secure climate. Hence collective provision must be at the heart of the good economy.

Resource depletion and climate change

The current phase of capitalism has driven us well beyond the limits of environmental sustainability. We face serious resource constraints. If everybody lived as we do in Europe we would need 3 planets to sustain us.[16] Climate change is perhaps the biggest security challenge faced by human kind.

We are reaching the end of low cost oil.[17] Demand is forecast to grow by 50 per cent by 2025. Some in OPEC say that oil supply will not be adequate to satisfy world demand in 15 years. At some stage we will reach an oil peak, after which the rate of world oil production will not increase. Many estimates suggest that this peak will arrive some time between 2010 and 2020, or potentially even sooner. Previous energy transitions (e.g. from wood to coal and coal to oil) were gradual. Case studies of regions and countries which have passed their own oil peak suggest, however, that even a year ahead of the event there was no sign that oil was about to peak. Oil peaking is not an energy crisis in the conventional sense – it is a liquid fuels problem. Cars, planes, trains and ships have no alternative to liquid fuels at the moment. Renewables and nuclear power create electricity rather than liquid fuel, and their widespread use in transport is far off. If we do not reduce demand for and dependence on motorised transport, we face severe economic hardship in the form of massive oil shortages.

There is now an overwhelming consensus among qualified scientists that humankind's greenhouse gas emissions need to be reduced drastically within years rather than decades to avert a big increase in the risk of unstoppable and catastrophic climate change. There are still uncertainties about precisely how much reduction is needed; and how responsibility for reductions should be shared out between countries is a matter for political negotiation. But there will be no chance of securing adequate commitments from the US, the current greatest threat to global climate security, and China and India whose rapid industrialisation poses future threats, unless and until currently high-consuming countries such the UK actually make substantial cuts. Government has set a target to reduce greenhouse gas emissions by 60 per cent by 2050. The latest climate research shows very strong evidence that markedly faster and deeper cuts even than this are needed for climate security.

The likelihood of catastrophic and irreversible climate change (e.g. the Greenland ice shelf melting, eventually raising sea levels by 7 metres) gets much worse if global temperatures rise more than 2 degrees (since pre-industrial times). This is likely to happen if atmospheric carbon concentration exceeds 400 parts per million. If emissions continue at present levels this will happen within 10 years. Given the timescales which policy interventions take to come into effect, it is the decisions made or avoided in the next few years – by the next elected Prime Minister of the UK and the next elected President of the US amongst others – which will determine whether climate change spirals out of control or not.

Even after recent price rises, energy is still historically cheap. Competition has driven down energy prices at the expense of cutting infrastructure investment and jeopardising future energy security. For most people and organisations, saving energy just is not worth the time and effort. Low prices have encouraged the continuation of inefficient habits. However for a minority on low incomes energy costs are already a serious threat to quality of life because of difficulty in affording fuel to keep energy-leaky homes warm, or to drive energy-inefficient vehicles to work.

Most of us are in the short term locked in to energy profligate habits and lifestyles. Many of the changes needed to make big reductions in energy use would cause serious inconvenience, disruption or even hardship in the short term. Consequently, exhortations to reduce energy use have limited practical effect, but cause considerable resentment at government for unrealistic buck passing. There are structural problems across the board. For example, landlords have little incentive to invest in energy efficiency because tenants reap the benefits; tenants are unwilling to invest in improvements on homes they do not own. In transport the focus on consumer choice has created a vicious circle. It is not possible for us to individually choose a good public transport system – such a choice needs to be made collectively through democracy.

Varieties of capitalism

The trends and pressures of contemporary capitalism can seem relentless and all-conquering, and have indeed proved a serious challenge to the realisation of the most progressive and ambitious aspects of the Labour government's programme. But the most important lesson of any review of today's world economy is that, for all these constraints and difficulties, it is still a world of genuine alternative paths.

The international trends and forces associated with financialisation have encouraged a universalisation of the neo-liberal model and a narrowing of the institutional differences once celebrated between different kinds of capitalism.[18] The shine is, however, coming off the neo-liberal model, which, for example in the United States, has led to very high levels of inequality, and is being resisted by many countries including those in Latin America. Even such mainstream voices as Lord Adair Turner, who headed the Pensions Commission, have stressed the range of socio-political choice that remains open in today's global economy;[19] and the Nordic economies continue to demonstrate the viability of a model that combines economic dynamism with a robust framework of redistributive egalitarianism.

Indeed the two major economies that are increasingly central to discussions of intensifying international competition, India and China, have developed their positions in the global economy through highly unorthodox and interventionist economic policies. The intensity of political struggles over the future of the social model in France and Germany demonstrate the power of popular support for basic social protections, while in Latin America even more radical challenges to the neo-liberal world order are gaining momentum. There is a growing awareness that the controls have been taken off the world economy, but also that we do have the power to re-regulate it – that these are political decisions not inevitable results.

In the UK, some policy analysts have claimed to detect an emerging 'Anglo-social model' in the efforts of the Labour government to combine labour flexibility and high rates of employment with a careful expansion of redistributive and universal provision.[20] It remains to be seen whether this new paradigm can be radicalised and augmented through a spirit of dialogue and collaboration with progressive social forces throughout Europe and around the world.

A new political economy

We need a step-change in policy if we are to begin to shape an economy that offers everyone a satisfying and rewarding role at the same time as recognising that there is much of value beyond the realm of formal employment and private monetary gain. What are the means by which we can strengthen the economy so that it becomes democratic and provides social justice, quality of life for all and environmental sustainability? To achieve these goals, imaginative action is needed in a number of key areas, and the remainder of this book considers the practical policies – ranging across areas such as energy, employment, housing, the national fiscal framework and the global economy – which can take us there.

3 A new economics

Narrow economic measures of the economy are inadequate. Economic policy needs rethinking in a number of ways. It must include proper measures of the value of non-market goods and services provided by the public sector and voluntary sector, and proper measures of the value of household services and the value of non-market time. We need to adjust the analysis of market efficiency to properly include the impact that market actions and transactions have on third parties not involved in the market transaction, such as environmental damage. We also should look at the impact of economic policies on the distribution of income, wealth and well-being, on 'happiness', and on environmental sustainability, rather than a narrow focus on maximising GDP.

Today's capitalist system, with its focus on maximising shareholder value, has a tendency to bias economic policy away from these wider concepts and towards narrower measures of economic efficiency. Not only is this tendency destructive of the good society, it is also inefficient in the wider economic sense.

Valuing the public and voluntary sectors and the household

The 'economy' is usually discussed in a relatively narrow sense that recognises only commercial institutions and relationships and monetary measures of income, production and wealth. We need a broader notion of economic activity and its context. As well as the private and public sector, the third sector and the household sector should also be considered. As well as goods and services sold on the market it is important to include goods and services that are provided free at point of service by state subsidy, or provided voluntarily. It is also crucial to consider the indirect impacts that economic activity can have on other agents in the economy who are not party to a transaction (what economists call 'externalities').

In the private sector, rival profit-seeking firms employ paid workers to produce goods and services for sale in markets. The public sector comprises both the state, narrowly defined in terms of basic government functions, and various tax-financed agencies directly controlled or set up by the state. These are normally, though not necessarily, non-profit-seeking, but in any case they employ paid workers to produce generally non-marketed services which are usually available to the general public free of charge or at a subsidised price. The third sector contains a variety of charities, membership organisations, civic associations, social enterprises, co-operatives and informal networks, which employ both paid staff and unpaid volunteers, to express shared values, promote shared interests and cater to social needs that are either not met at all, or not met so well, by commercial, public or domestic providers. They may be partially funded by contracts with the state but usually also rely on individual donations and/or grants from charitable bodies. There are of course many hybrid institutions and forms which cross between these three sectors – for example public-private partnerships – but together these three sectors make up the 'paid' or 'formal economy'. The 'unpaid' or 'informal economy' consists of the household and community sectors, within which individuals perform unpaid provisioning and caring work both for themselves and for the benefit of those with whom they live and others in their community. Again there can be some straddling of the divide between the paid and unpaid economies. For example, third sector organisation may have both unpaid volunteers and salaried employees.

Economies are embedded in our broader ecosystem. Issues such as climate change and resource depletion mean that there is a need to be aware of the feedback systems between the environment we live in and the economic activity we engage in. Taking this wider picture of the whole economy leads to a different and richer perspective. It means the challenge is not simply to prioritise the economy of private business, but to look after the wider economy as a whole and the environment in which it is embedded, and to look for an appropriate balance between its interdependent elements.

Today's economic policy debate is driven by a focus on a range of goals – economic growth, efficiency, high levels of employment, investment and productivity – with policy-makers often focusing only on the paid economy and ignoring effects on the unpaid economy. For example, current GDP growth rates are inflated by a movement from the unpaid to the paid economy, which must in the long run be unsustainable. Such goals should not be valued as ends in themselves, but to the extent that they promote quality of life and social justice in a framework of environmental sustainability.

Rethinking economic concepts

Taking a wider notion of the economy and thinking about environmental sustainability, social justice and well-being mean that traditional economic concepts need to be rethought.

Efficiency is usually taken to be a desirable goal, but there is a question of what we are making efficient. An economy that produces cheap food but at a cost of ill-health and environmental damage is inefficient. An efficient childcare centre is one with a low ratio of staff to children, which is usually taken as a measure of poor quality. Conservative and Labour governments have both made claims as to the superior 'efficiency' of private sector providers of public services, but evidence indicates that a large portion of their cost-savings are achieved not through improved management and utilisation of labour but by making staff work longer hours for lower pay.[21] We need to measure efficiency against the values we are promoting.

Similarly, although employment is very often desirable and usually better than unemployment, moving into employment can sometimes take people out of the household economy or volunteering for the third sector, and this may not be a good thing, especially if they are moved into low quality employment. As research has argued, 'a policy which reduces financial hardship (improving satisfaction with income) by giving the poor access to jobs which involve long hours and poor conditions, is likely to have off-setting effects in the domains of satisfaction with work, health, friends and family relationships'.[22] There may be no net gain in well-being, and possibly a net loss, if the care economy is sacrificed to the work economy.

The traditional notion of investment can also be challenged. For example, the Chancellor's Golden Rule – that he will balance current account spending and revenue over the economic cycle and borrow only to invest (to fund capital spending) – is said to look after the interests of future generations by ensuring that they will have to repay only the costs of investment from which they themselves will benefit.

However, this distinction between investment and current account spending is not the same as a distinction between the kinds of spending that benefit future citizens and those that benefit citizens today. Contributions to the human capital (in practice made disproportionately by women) of future generations, especially in the fields of care, health and education, are allocated to current spending, while contributions to physical infrastructure projects (in practice made disproportionately by men) are more likely to count as capital spending. The former are constrained by the Golden Rule, while the latter counts as investment, with borrowing therefore allowed for their finance. This rule results in a distortion of public spending – away from 'current account' spending that benefits future generations through raising their human capital, including caring, and towards forms of investment in physical capital that forms part of the 'capital account'. Borrowing to finance 'current account' spending on projects of value to future generations is not permitted. This results in over-investment in physical capital and under-investment in human capital. We need to rebalance this skew of expenditure, by including spending on human capital in the capital account.

Measures of productivity also need challenging. It is increasingly recognised that productivity measures need to be treated with care. For example the US is very productive on a per capita basis, but not so productive when compared on measures which look at productivity per hour worked. But there are other reasons to be careful of productivity measures. Productivity may not be a desirable measure in all industries. For example, in caring, education and some other personal services high productivity can rarely be achieved without lowering quality. That is why the staff/client ratio tends to be used as a measure of quality. A focus on productivity might increase Gross Value Added (GVA) but could reduce well-being in other respects. For example, many businesses are run on the basis of creating fulfilling work for the owners and/or workers and a public benefit for their community. Further, the ruthless pursuit of productivity can also conflict with environmental concerns. Finally, a pure focus on productivity can be inconsistent with increased social inclusion or an enterprise approach to regenerating disadvantaged areas. As more people with low and intermediate skills enter the workforce, this may reduce average productivity. Individuals who have not traditionally been in mainstream employment tend to be less productive in terms of output per head than the core workforce. Indeed this is something that goes towards explaining the UK's low productivity levels: an insistence on a low national minimum wage has allowed the government to focus on bringing excluded people into the labour market rather than on improving the quality and productivity of the jobs that are available to them.

Well-being and balanced growth

There is an increasing sense of divergence between material affluence and the quality of people's lives. One of the main ways this is felt is in terms of the loss of the public realm which has accompanied the growth of individual incomes, something which is explored in more detail in *Democracy and the Public Realm*. In the public realm we experience those things which are produced and used collectively by society: things whose experience is not individual to us, but which we share with our neighbours. Our environment is a key part of the public realm. Culture, public services and the absence of crime are other examples of things which are public goods which affect our well-being even if we have individual material affluence. For example the fear of crime makes us fear strangers and be suspicious of our neighbours. It depopulates town centres and public spaces. The poor are the biggest victims of most types of crime, but even if we are well off, crime makes us socially poorer.

There are diminishing marginal returns in terms of well-being to material comfort. For individuals above a basic material threshold, relative levels of income are far more important for well-being than absolute levels of income: we compare ourselves to others and we also adjust to our new levels of comfort very quickly.[23] And societally we now seem to be at the stage where the processes which create economic growth can simultaneously decrease well-being. For example, in the UK for most of the twentieth century time spent in paid employment fell from more than 50 hours a week to around 35, but this trend was stalled and partially reversed in the 1980s.[24] Despite some reductions since the late 1990s, recent data confirms that, apart from Latvia, UK full-time employees still work the longest weekly hours in the EU.[25] We have by far the largest proportion working excess hours, with one in seven (and one in three fathers) putting in more than 48 hours a week. This might be explained by the desire to increase relative income. There is, however, a collective action problem: if we all work longer hours, and it is only relative levels of income that determine happiness, there will be no net increase in well-being (as we will all remain roughly where we were in the hierarchy of relative income). In fact we might expect a net decrease in well-being, as people work so hard they have less time for their families, friends, communities and hobbies, or to look after their own health. Further, increased incomes from high working hours will help bid up the price of commodities which are scarce – land for housing is the most important example of this. This means that average mortgage payments rise, which leads to longer working hours to make the payment, which bids up the price of housing and so on.

For people on low incomes a principal contributor to a higher quality of life would be a higher income. Nevertheless there is today a very tangible sense that for many of those more comfortably off within society, raising private incomes should no longer be the only political objective for governments. Higher individual incomes do not guarantee greater well-being, either for individuals or for society at large.

These insights dramatically re-orientate progressive politics in two ways. First private incomes are not a sufficient measure of quality of life. The principal need today is for spending on public goods and higher taxation must be paid to secure them. This may reduce (or, more likely, slow the growth of) private consumption, but increase well-being. The second implication is that societies should not measure their success by the traditional measure of economic growth. Economic growth should be valued not as an end in itself – but insofar as it provides a sustainable and socially just route to a better quality of life. We should focus attention on what kind of growth and development we want to see, and what trade-offs we are prepared to make as a society as we engage in economic production – just as individuals seek to make choices about the kind of career they want to pursue and the balance they seek to strike between their earnings and other valued aspects of their lives.

We need to seek balanced growth which promotes well-being, social justice and environmental sustainability. We need to think more about the distribution of the costs and benefits of economic growth, and whether the costs should be allowed to lie where they fall – on the weakest members of society – migrants, women, carers, the unemployed and the poor. This can tie into a range of other agendas, including quality of working life, making sure that people are well cared for and sustainable consumption. It therefore becomes a vital task to identify alternative indicators and measures which more accurately represent the full dimensions of well-being and quality of life.

We need an expansive framework of national accounts, based on the multi-dimensional model of the economy outlined earlier in the chapter, so as to bring the social and environmental aspects of economic policy more fully into view. Using this national accounts framework, policy should aim at maximising wider measures of well-being rather than maximising GDP, the aim of so much of current policy. We need to achieve this through better national and local indicators of progress. In particular, national accounts ought to contain measures of our environmental assets (a 'balance sheet'). GDP could also be adjusted for social and environmental effects, to give a better view of how we are faring as a society[26] (although we accept that it is not possible to put a 'true' financial value on environmental systems.) This is something that a number of Regional Development Agencies (RDAs) are presently experimenting with.

We could better capture the value of unpaid work in the household and community through the further development of the statistics that are captured nationally on this in what are called the 'household satellite accounts'.[27] And we should directly measure people's well-being in terms of a range of subjective and objective indicators – something which the Department for Environment, Food and Rural Affairs is currently exploring. All of these issues, on which government agencies are doing welcome work, need to become a greater part of the mainstream debate.

New measures of progress need to be complemented with the reform of processes such as regulatory impact assessment and cost benefit analysis so that they take account of impacts and cuts wherever they fall and address the distributional issues which are currently seen as marginal. And we need new measures of social and environmental value to enter the marketplace to help shape better transactions.[28] As Al Gore has said, 'we are operating planet earth as if it is a business in liquidation. We really do have to modify the way we measure, recognise and deal with value inside the market system so that it takes into account the values that are what humanity is all about.'[29]

All of these things would allow us to understand better the trade-offs between different sectors of the economy, and to maximise real prosperity and quality of life. For example an expansion of the formal economy can be at the expense of uncounted social activities and experiences located in the household or third sectors.[30] We are not optimising economic policy if we do not recognise the costs it gives rise to in the unpaid economy. For example, pressuring parents to work longer hours, as employers are able to do under the UK government's opt-out from the EU Working Time Directive, comes at the cost of less time being available for caring and community activities and for leisure too, which can be bad for the well-being both of parents and their children..

None of the above is to say that using traditional economic concepts is a bad idea. But these concepts are valuable to the extent that they are used to create the economy we value. They are not ends in themselves and we should not pursue them as if they are. We need to reshape the way we think about economic progress by assessing everything we do in terms of its impact on well-being, social justice and environmental sustainability. This is the way to create a dynamic, innovative and prosperous society.

4 The challenge of sustainability

Nowhere is the notion of a political economy more important than environmental sustainability and climate change. The dominant free market political economy is taking us to the final boom and bust – that of the planet. We have to stop it now.

As outlined in chapter 2, big reductions in global greenhouse gas emissions need to be achieved – not just promised or talked about – within years rather than decades. Climate change is a national security threat and needs to be treated with the urgency and seriousness that terrorism has been. Rapid UK emissions reduction is certainly not sufficient for climate security, but it is necessary as a prerequisite for global security. As the Stern Review argues, it will be more costly to deal with climate change the later we leave it.[31] It is a sensible economic decision to deal with climate change now, and it will also help us build innovation which will allow us to be leaders in environmental markets.

Some level of climate change is now inevitable. Stopping global temperatures from rising 2 degrees centigrade is still possible. Even an increase of 2 degrees would have major negative economic, social and environmental impacts for all countries. Anything above this increases further damage much more rapidly and increases the likelihood of catastrophic damage. Keeping to a 2 degree rise requires year-on-year cuts in the UK's carbon dioxide emissions of at least 3 per cent a year. Other rich countries will need to do the same. Doing this will require major changes to taxes, spending and regulations to give businesses and individuals the incentives to cut their emissions in a way which benefits the economy and increases people's quality of life. Action on climate change is not just a moral imperative but essential now to the short and long term future economic and social well-being of the people in the UK. Research shows that there is no link between consumption and life satisfaction once basic needs are met. This implies that we could move towards more sustainable levels of consumption and potentially increase the quality of our lives.

We need to dispose of a number of myths which are currently providing a pretext for government complacency, and pursuit of irrelevant actions rather than necessary ones. The first myth is that the UK is already successfully dealing with climate change. It is true that the UK, almost uniquely among rich countries, has reduced greenhouse gas emissions substantially since 1990, and appears to be on target to achieve its Kyoto Protocol target. However the decline was largely an accidental byproduct of the replacement of coal by gas (which releases far less CO_2 per unit of energy released) and to the decline of energy-intensive manufacturing industry.

The 'dash for gas' has now stopped, and may indeed need to be reversed in order to reduce the UK's dangerous vulnerability to geopolitical turmoil in gas-producing ex-Soviet countries – a direct consequence of the UK having squandered its gas reserves. The decline of UK manufacturing did not actually reduce the emissions for which the UK is responsible, but merely transferred them 'off balance sheet'. In other words they are chalked up to the greenhouse gas accounts of the countries which now manufacture the goods we still consume, but which we now import instead of making ourselves. So even if the UK continued to close down what is left of its manufacturing sector, the apparent reduction in greenhouse emissions would be an illusion. Critics of China's rapidly growing energy consumption and greenhouse emissions should remember that these are largely incurred making products for consumption in the rich parts of the world.

Now these two windfalls are over, emissions are rising again. Moreover, emissions due to air travel – the most environmentally damaging mode of transport per passenger kilometre, but one where the government is encouraging rapid growth – are excluded from the Kyoto protocol and from most published climate change statistics. Therefore, the UK's two windfalls have encouraged a belief that the UK's market-based approach is an enviably painless and effective way to reduce greenhouse emissions. In fact the windfalls have only temporarily masked the reality that emissions are continuing to increase, and the UK's current policies will at best slow the growth.

The second myth is one based on 'resource productivity' – let the market drive technical innovation to get more economic benefit from each unit of environmental consumption (including fossil fuel). This fits the discourses around modernisation, competitiveness, innovation and entrepreneurship favoured by government.

The market does drive efficiency improvements. But it is financial productivity that the market drives. This only lines up with environmental resource productivity where the environmental resource or damage carries a high market price. Currently it is usually cheap or free, so companies can often get better productivity gains by using more environmental goods, if this enables them to save on other, more expensive, factors of production. For example, 'just in time' ordering, manufacturing and delivery reduces working capital tied up in inventories, and the risk of having to write off unsold stock, at the expense of increased road (and sometimes) air freight movements, and consequent greenhouse emissions, which do not have to be paid for.

Resource productivity improvements are neutralised by 'rebound' effects. Houses became far more energy efficient between 1970 and 2000, but energy consumption per household stayed exactly the same, because people responded to the efficiency improvements (and drop in the real price of energy relative to incomes) by heating more space to high temperatures for longer periods, buying bigger energy consuming appliances, and being more careless about turning them off when not wanted. Likewise, the average fuel efficiency of new cars sold stayed the same from 1984 to 2000 because consumers responded to fuel efficiency improvements by buying bigger, heavier, higher performance vehicles. Hence eco-efficiency cannot be relied on to reduce consumption unless combined with policy measures to counteract rebound effects.

The third myth is that new technology will rescue us. There are two problems with this. First, novel technologies (nuclear fusion, carbon capture) are speculative and uncertain, or have big downsides of their own. Hydrogen is only an energy carrier: it can reduce pollution and increase efficiency at the point of use, but is no cleaner over all than the method used to generate it. Hydrogen from renewable power would be an advance (though no more of one than electricity or heat from renewables). But hydrogen produced from natural gas still emits carbon and depletes a scarce high quality fuel. The second issue is that we already have technologies which could transform our emissions. The problem is that we do not apply them. The reasons are institutional and political, not technological. Developing new technologies is a distraction from dealing with the reasons we do not apply the technologies we already have.

Principles and measures

What are the principles that should guide our energy system?[32] The Government's energy review is right to argue that climate change, energy security and affordable warmth should be cardinal goals of energy policy. The review's support for energy efficiency, distributed generation, combined heat and power and renewables is to be welcomed. But its reliance on persuasion, information and a bewildering plethora of intricate financial incentives and market-based mechanisms masks a continued failure of will to intervene adequately and effectively. Indeed the failure is made clear by the energy review's own heavy reliance on increasing fossil fuel imports from politically volatile regions, supplemented by a new generation of nuclear power stations. The review proposes to enable a new generation of nuclear through bypassing the democratic scrutiny and planning procedures which currently allow consideration of the costs, safety risks and environmental damage of nuclear power.

Climate security and energy security both require rapid reductions in fossil fuel without resorting to new nuclear power. These goals can be reconciled with well-being (including affordable warmth for all) provided government takes political responsibility for managing markets.

Four principles should guide our approach:

Energy services
Nobody wants to consume energy as such. What we actually want is services which energy can provide: warmth, light, washing, cooking, operation of equipment and appliances, travel and so on. The prime focus of energy policy should be to reduce the amount of energy needed to provide these services. Improving the technical efficiency of energy-using equipment is only one way to achieve this – and one, moreover, which is largely ineffectual on its own because it reduces the cost, which encourages people to use more energy services (the 'rebound effect').

Obviation
Obviation – simply avoiding the need for energy – is often more effective than efficiency. There are huge opportunities to provide the services people need without buying energy. Intelligent design and layout can minimise the need for energy for heating and lighting in houses and many other buildings. Intelligent spatial planning can greatly reduce the amount people need to travel to access amenities.

Behaviour change and decision points
Energy policy is still based on the myth that people go around rationally calculating the costs and benefits every time we buy a loaf of bread, get in the car or turn on a light, and that we will respond instantly to every little change in price or snippet of information on energy efficiency. In fact we are creatures of habit: in most departments of life we carry on doing what we always done, saving our cognitive powers for things we really care about, until actively jolted out of our rut. It is therefore not enough just to set a background framework of incentives to save energy (although necessary): policy needs to provide these jolts if we want people to change their habits on what for them are unimportant background issues. A number of environmental policy recommendations in *The Good Society* were of these kind – designed to unfreeze behaviour patterns.

Most people are locked in to life routines and consequent patterns of energy use, and can only make significant changes when we make major life changes such as moving house or job. Policy needs to make sure that energy figures at these decision points.

Just transition
As discussed in the next chapter, a sustainability programme should link to industrial policy, and focus upon job creation, and a just transition programme

for workers who may lose jobs in industries which are hit by the transition towards sustainability.

This chapter considers policy to deal with the major climate challenges that we face in relation to energy and transport, based on the principles outlined above.

Steady, predictable increases in the real cost of energy and smart tariffs

Depletion of the technically easiest reserves, geopolitical turmoil, climate related disruption and increased global competition mean the age of cheap energy is over. Prices are going to rise and keep rising whether we like it or not. Current attempts to disguise the underlying realities by deferring or reducing energy taxation and putting pressure on energy suppliers to absorb price increases are cowardly and counterproductive. Instead, government should acknowledge that rising energy prices are inevitable and help everyone acknowledge, understand and plan for this; ease and enable the transition to a radically lower carbon way of life (in particular through making homes more energy efficient – see chapter 8); and safeguard vulnerable people from suffering. Energy tax levels should be at least maintained, and generally increased year on year, to give a clear motivation to change behaviour; to fund measures to support transition to a low carbon economy; and to provide a margin of manoeuvre for action to offset short-term instabilities and shocks. For example temporary tax reductions could be used to insulate consumers from short-term 'spikes' due, for example, to natural disasters or terrorist successes.

Energy suppliers should be required to sell every household enough energy to meet basic needs at a low price. This could be cross-subsidised out of higher prices charged for energy above basic needs, or through block purchasing by the government.[33] The amount of energy each household can buy at the basic needs tariff would be based on the energy performance of each dwelling, modified by any special needs of the household (for example those of very young, very old or disabled members). This could be coupled with incentives to improve energy efficiency.

This system will virtually abolish fuel poverty, by allowing all households to meet basic energy needs at a low price. It is progressively redistributive, because it cross-subsidises a low rate which will cover a larger proportion of poorer households' consumption out of higher rates paid by wealthier consumers for discretionary consumption. It gives all households a stronger incentive to save energy. It also gives energy suppliers a commercial incentive to support energy conservation measures, to minimise the amount of energy they are obliged to sell at low, indeed potentially loss-making, rates.

A decentralised energy system

At present a few power stations generate electricity and transmit it where it is needed, often hundreds of miles away. A huge amount of energy – around two thirds – is lost by this system as heat. We need to move towards a decentralised energy system in which most electricity is generated by Combined Heat and Power stations and micro-generators close to where it is needed, and where most of the heat can also be used, so there is far less energy loss.[34] Decentralised energy would be a major step in meeting energy needs. It would also give citizens a more active stake in energy policy: micro-generation is shown to make people more interested in where energy comes from and where it is used – especially when they are able to produce a surplus of electricity and sell it back to the grid! A decentralised system is already being used in some areas in Britain such as Woking, and some European cities, such as Rotterdam, Malmo and Helsinki, have adopted decentralised energy systems. Government commissioned research shows that moving to a decentralised energy system will not be hugely expensive, and in fact could lead to lower cost electricity.[35]

Renewables, coal and nuclear

As discussed in the next chapter, part of our approach to energy must be to increase the role of renewable energy, including wind, wave, tidal, solar and biomass. There need to be fiscal incentives to do this, and a better planning framework to prevent delays in decision making. As part of the transition to a decentralised and renewable energy system there is a role for clean coal. Carbon capture and storage can reduce emissions by up to 85 per cent. Therefore this needs to be developed in sufficient time to use clean coal power stations as a transition technology.

Nuclear power is a low carbon technology which could generate lots of electricity. But the Government's own sustainable development watchdog has made the case that nuclear power is not necessary for energy security.[36] Even if the UK's nuclear capacity were doubled, it would only give an 8 per cent cut in carbon emissions by 2035. In the meantime a new generation of nuclear power would lock the UK into a centralised energy system – the experience of Finland shows that a new nuclear generation gets in the way from moving to a decentralised and renewable system, which is what is necessary. And perhaps the biggest risk with nuclear power is that there are no available long-term solutions to dealing with nuclear waste, creating major safety risks. The cost of nuclear power is also high and unquantified. Whilst government has maintained that there will be no public subsidy for any new plants, it is clear that there are risks that costs may fall on the taxpayer. On balance the risks associated with a new generation of nuclear power generators outweigh the benefits in terms of carbon emissions. Therefore the government should not proceed with nuclear power as part of its energy strategy and instead invest its resources and political capital to take forward the other strategies outlined here.

Transport for sustainability

Transport is one of the largest sources of greenhouse gas emissions, and one of the hardest to tackle. The underlying reasons are political. Effective intervention has been hamstrung by the false belief that allowing maximum freedom of individual choice must inevitably achieve the best collective result, and by reliance on uncoordinated piecemeal initiatives which have little effect in isolation.

Most businesses prefer locations with good parking and road connections because most customers and employees (especially the wealthier and higher qualified ones) prefer to come by car. For years spatial planning has promoted urban locations and parking restraint, but planners know that if they push these too far they will simply lose development to other places. Many bus services are heavily subsidised to promote transport 'choice'. But while journey patterns are highly fragmented (because employers and others choose sites with good parking which are usually away from other destinations), the only people who will 'choose' these buses are those with no choice. Cycle and pedestrian facilities are used largely by minorities sufficiently committed to defy the logistical and social obstacles. It is politically very difficult to penalise, restrict or even discourage car use as most people rely on cars to get access to what they want in life.

Many continental cities show that it does not have to be like this. It is possible to have a virtuous circle in which trip generators (e.g. employers or shops) are happy to be in urban centres because that is where their users already are, or can easily go, and where public transport provides a good service to concentrated destinations, and is therefore well used, which in turn provides the revenue to keep the services good. In such situations shorter journeys reward and encourage cycling and walking, which remain 'normal': routine activities done by normal people as part of their daily routine in ordinary clothes without elaborate special equipment. These cities tend to have heavy restrictions on car use (including complete vehicle bans over large areas, streets where pedestrians take precedence and vehicles must move at walking pace, restricted parking with high charges, etc), and these are taken for granted as 'groundrules' of decent civilised life.

The policy challenge for the UK is to flip from the vicious to the virtuous circle. This is easiest to achieve in new settlements or urban quarters. All new settlements and extensions should be designed car free, with high quality amenities within the 'pedshed', excellent public transport to urban centres and active discouragement of car use.

It is harder to achieve the same result in existing settlements because of the need for a step change in several interdependent aspects of life together. Existing cities and towns should be encouraged and supported to make a planned step change to low transport demand, with coordinated action to transform the quality of public transport, ensure local amenities are high quality, and actively restrict car use. Congestion should be tackled by road pricing. This should be additional to fuel taxes, because the aim should also be to reduce traffic over all, not merely spread it out as congestion charging might do. There should be more commitment to grow the railways, and local authorities should be given the power to re-regulate bus services.

Finally, there is the issue of air travel. Air travel is more fuel intensive than any other transport mode per passenger kilometre. Moreover, the over-all climate change impacts of air travel are estimated to be between 2 and 4 times greater than the fuel consumption implies because of the effects of emissions in the upper atmosphere. Air travel already accounts for about 10-14 per cent of the UK's total climate change impacts. If current trends continue this would rise to about 40 per cent by 2050 – in other words air travel would take up all the emissions the UK would be allowed if the target of a 60 per cent reduction by 2050 were to be met.

It is absurd to plan for a major increase in these emissions, which would undo the benefits sought from cuts in all other sectors. Government should plan for the same 60 per cent reduction in climate change impacts from air travel by 2050 as it is already seeking for all other sectors. Air travel should not be exempt from the agreements and disciplines which affect all other emissions: it should be included in all national and international climate change agreements and targets. Air fuel should be taxed on the same basis as other petroleum products. We should not be building new airports, which create as well as meet demand. We should also auction landing slots – a per landing charge is far less regressive than a per passenger charge.

Complaints that these measures would deprive poorer people of the freedom to fly are unsubstantiated. Air travel is still disproportionately the realm of the better off. Authoritative recent research shows that 76 per cent of leisure passengers were from socio economic groups ABC1 and only 24 per cent from C2DE. It also shows that in the period 2000-2004 'the number of international leisure trips by UK residents in the lower two household income bands has fallen ... an absolute fall of approximately 2 million one-way trips per year ... meanwhile the total number of international leisure trips made by UK residents has increased by a total of more than 7 million one way trips per year.'[37] In other words, it is overwhelmingly rich people who fly, and the recent falls in the cost of flying have simply meant rich people fly more, rather than opening up flying for poorer people. Poorer people fly less than 5 years ago. The aim of policy should be to increase the ability of the poorest to afford air travel, as well as other luxuries, by redistributive policies to reduce Britain's extremes of income and wealth insecurity. At the same time policy needs to make air travel more expensive compared to other luxuries to reflect its environmental damage. The way to address social injustice is not by making things artificially and damagingly cheap, but to radically redistribute so that no one is poor.

The environment sustains us – without it there can be no economy. We need to make major changes to the way our economy is run so as to meet the environmental challenges we face. This can be done in a way that can promote our well-being and lessen inequalities, to create a progressive and prosperous political economy.

5 The promise of a knowledge economy

In the 1990s many seized upon the notion of a 'knowledge economy' as a route to creating a prosperous economy that embodied progressive values of well-being, social justice and environmental sustainability.[38] As a result of both globalisation and technological advance, markets were placing increasing value on skills, innovation, information, and creativity. This meant that jobs were becoming inherently more fulfilling and enjoyable, as firms responded to the new environment, while progressive governments could develop new justificatory rationales for public spending on education and other services as business-friendly investments in human and social 'capital'. In this new 'weightless' or 'frictionless' world, paid work was becoming increasingly painless and the economy increasingly free of social and political conflict. The knowledge economy seemed to provide government with a way to protect the population from the worst excesses of the labour-cost-cutting global competition, through getting out of low skilled jobs.

It is an appealing story, and one that is not entirely without foundation. There is evidence to indicate that in many economies, especially those of the OECD, the share of national income and employment accounted for by 'knowledge-based' activities (however that is defined) is increasing.[39] This trend may be related to the increasing share of world manufacturing that is now located in newly industrialising countries with lower labour costs. More fundamentally, it might be seen as an underlying secular trend consequent upon technological progress – as physical production processes become increasingly automated, a greater proportion of human labour time is devoted to more intellectual, analytical, creative, communicative, interactive and emotional activities.

This shift has for many been epitomised and accelerated by the information and communications revolutions of recent decades, which permeates and undergirds many other phenomena associated with this trend – such as the relative growth of service sectors from entertainment to hospitality, the emergence of new science-led industries such as microelectronics and biopharmaceuticals, and the increasing insertion of high-tech design and production processes throughout manufacturing and engineering.

And there is no doubt that these areas of the economy have the potential to offer more rewarding, empowering, and participative ways of working for those employed in them, at the same time as improving and enriching life for all in exciting new ways. The image of the 'knowledge economy' has thus become a shorthand for evoking capitalism's ability to deliver ongoing technological advance and productivity gains.

The problem with the knowledge economy utopia is not that the idea is unattractive, but that it remains a long way from reality. Today's knowledge economy has yet to extend beyond the limits of relatively privileged zones of the economy, or segments of the labour market; its benefits and attractions are out of reach for large sections of our society, not to mention humanity at large.[40] Partly this is a matter of inhibiting institutional contexts and inadequate levels of investment and support at all levels. High skill jobs are high productivity jobs and therefore it takes a greater level of initial investment to create a given number of such jobs than it does to create low productivity ones. Partly it is because the 'knowledge economy' itself depends upon social contexts and production processes which are often overlooked and undervalued – such as the all-important 'care economy' discussed in the next chapter, or the labour that goes into the manufacture and maintenance of information, communication and transport systems (computer chipmaking, for example, has one of the highest instances of occupational injury and illness in the US).[41]

But it is also because today's knowledge economy is being constructed to meet the alleged requirement to compete in the global marketplace, rather than the social and human needs upon which it is premised. This means that precisely as the new knowledge economy is being built, its attractions are at risk of being neutralised, as education and information is commodified, science and culture are commercialised, and ways of relating are re-routinised and re-hierarchised. The advance of the knowledge economy can be a double-edged process – from one point of view an incorporation of human values and democratic practices into the market economy, but from another point of view the marketisation of activities and areas of social life that had previously constituted separate and relatively autonomous domains.

We must recognise that the knowledge economy is dependent upon public support and wider social processes, and in turn must ensure that the knowledge economy works in the public interest and to meet social needs.

The foundations of a knowledge economy

The first step in articulating a new approach must be a recognition that, despite the habitual (and sometimes deliberate) linking of new technologies and ways of working with other predominant features of the new capitalism such as flexibility and financialisation, the relationships among these trends are complex and often contradictory. In fact, much of the evidence and experience suggests that obsessive deregulation, indiscriminate liberalisation and dependence upon the whims of globalised capital markets inhibits rather than promotes development of many of the phenomena celebrated by knowledge-economy enthusiasts. It is notable, for example, that the internet was essentially created by the US defence department: it is unlikely that it would ever have emerged from the market as it required so much investment. This is true for much infrastructure investment upon which knowledge economies are based, including telephone networks, railroads and energy.

In the UK, private capital markets drive firms to maximise financial gain, not to invest in skills, knowledge and technology.[42] This keeps the majority of British firms on the 'low road' of profitability through cost-cutting and labour-shedding, militating against the kind of organisational learning and strategic capacity development that is the necessary foundation of real innovation.[43] The UK still lags behind other major economies in terms of investment in technology, skills and R&D, and consequently in the productivity stakes when measured as output per hour worked. According to a recent OECD study the UK has shown 'a long-term decline in its relative innovation performance', with success in sectors based upon life sciences and chemistry, but 'a poor record in industries based on design-driven/engineering-based technologies'. It concludes that 'UK firms need to switch from a strategy of competing via cost-cutting and efficiency to one based on investment in innovation and generation of high value-added products.'[44]

The TUC has convincingly demonstrated that the UK suffers from a shortage of 'High Performance Workplaces', in part because of a short-sighted resistance on the part of both managers and government to grant employees improvements in job security and workplace representation. Even those companies operating in 'high value-added' markets have shown a tendency to restrict the majority of employees to 'a relatively narrow range of tasks, with limited job autonomy and little real involvement in work.'[45] Rightly, much emphasis has been laid upon the centrality of raising the education and skill levels of the UK workforce through 'supply-side measures'. But it is increasingly recognised that such measures need to be combined with strategies for tackling the low level of employer demand for skills and encouraging corporate strategies that can release the full potential of employee capacities.[46] Most jobs being created in the UK are at the low skill service end of the economy, and this implies that focusing purely on building human capital and skills is a limited strategy – it needs to be complemented by better employment protection, a higher level minimum wage and active trade unions.

Other countries with successful and growing knowledge-based sectors have benefited from proactive policies to encourage and support investment in cutting edge research and technology. US firms benefit from the channelling of massive federal investment into business-oriented research and development through a plethora of university institutes, which stimulates further R&D investment in the private sector.[47] Scandinavian countries such as Finland and Sweden, with their high levels of state spending, consistently appear near the top of the World Economic Forum's 'Networked Readiness Index', which measures the degree of preparation to participate in and benefit from ICT developments. Only Finland and Sweden have met the Lisbon agenda goal of devoting 3 per cent of GDP to Research and Development, with the UK spending only 1.9 per cent and planning an increase to 2.5 per cent in 2014. Manufacturing sectors in France and Germany remain highly productive, and are now driving both economies' recovery. In Germany this is in part due to a banking system that helps to provide long-term financial support for productive investment, while France has developed imaginative ways of stimulating growth in strategic areas, such as a proposed Industrial Innovation Agency, which would support investment in key sectors such as communications and nanotechnology.

Manufacturing in the UK, as with other western industrialised states, has undergone a massive shift in terms of sectors and employment as the globalisation of markets and production has developed. It is a key part of the knowledge economy. It is notable that the manufacturing sector accounts for 77 per cent of the total research and development expenditure in the UK.[48] Intensive labour based sectors have diminished in all but the more specialist targeted, high-added-value markets, and the future of manufacturing now lies in more highly skilled, knowledge based environments such as aerospace, pharmaceuticals, electronics and bio-technology. The nature of these industries is such that they are less labour intensive and demand a different skill set to the industries they are replacing. Manufacturing employment levels are, however, half those of 1997 – with employment figures now just over 3 million. The sector's share of GDP has fallen from 23 per cent in 1979 to 15 per cent in 2005.[49] However, the gross value added in manufacturing in 2005 was £148 billion, almost 20 per cent higher than in 1979.

There is a need to focus on the delivery of the necessary skills to enable UK manufacturing to compete in terms of productivity with the rest of Europe and further afield. Government policy in the UK does recognise the need to address the future skill needs of manufacturing. As argued in more detail in chapter 7, however, the practical application of that policy continues to fail industry by poor targeting of funding, complex bureaucracy of delivery and inadequate investment from employers. Recent attempts to redress the balance of our education system to deliver the vocational and science based skills necessary to sustain manufacturing in a global economy would seem to be too little, too late.

The challenge of environmentalism has strengthened, rather than undermined, the case for a new focus on industrial policy and sustainable job creation. The government in Denmark has worked within EU state aid rules to support the development of a world-class environmental industry that is a major supplier of wind-turbines. In the UK the environmental technology industry already provides 400,000 jobs with many more being created by the development of renewable energy sectors. The oil company Shell has estimated that over the next decade there are opportunities for Britain to have a £30 billion share of the market to develop technologies, products and services to combat climate change.[50]

In the UK, an industrial policy agenda on sustainable development would include development of the role of Innovation and Growth Teams in promoting strategic thinking and discussion about the future of key sectors, support for enterprises that can advance social and environmental goals through workspace subsidies and community finance initiatives, and ensuring a level playing field with other economies when it comes to support for industry through state aid and procurement policy.

It is important that environmental policies are developed with industrial policies in mind and vice versa, and that there is a just transition programme for workers for any job losses in those industries that may suffer as a result of a move towards sustainable development. It should be noted, however, that sustainability provides a real opportunity. For example decentralised and community-based energy and renewables offer skilled employment opportunities, and across a wider range of sites than centralised plants, which provide a relatively small and concentrated source of employment. In Germany there are five jobs in the renewables sector for every one job previously in the nuclear industry. As argued in the previous chapter, we need to invest in a decentralised energy system and renewables to build employment and move towards more sustainable development.

All these considerations suggest that the development of a successful knowledge economy depends less upon cutthroat competition and the maximisation of shareholder value, and more upon institutions that foster creativity and collaborative learning, and public support for investment in the knowledge, skills and technologies that will be at the heart of our economic future. To its credit, the Labour government has recognised much of this, and has taken valuable steps towards moving the UK onto a more progressive development path – by increasing investment in education and science, beginning to repair the public infrastructure, and making modest moves in the direction of a more regulated labour market. But it has remained too wedded to a laissez-faire rhetoric that overplays the role of private entrepreneurialism and underplays the contributions of public action and collective labour processes, and is too unwilling in practice to make tough choices and take on the vested interests that stand between us and a knowledge economy that lives up to the hype.

A knowledge economy for all

To this extent, the needs of the knowledge economy can reinforce and cohere with the aspiration for more fulfilling work and a more social economy. But there are dangers here as well as opportunities. For there are also signs that current knowledge-based economic strategies run the risk of distorting social goals and entrenching new forms of exclusion.

A key location for the emergence of these new contradictions is the university. Traditionally a site for the free pursuit of knowledge and articulation of humanist values, publicly disseminated through open publication and merit-based education, the university is now increasingly harnessed to economic, industrial and corporate strategies. In the US, where this process in many ways is most advanced, we have seen the subordination of academic and intellectual values to corporate and commercial imperatives.[51] This shows the pervasive impact upon both the content and the distribution of the knowledge and education that universities produce. In the UK these problems were laid bare by the debate over tuition fees – in order to match US spending on research and development, higher education in the UK is being turned over to the free market, resulting in a widely remarked commodification of education itself and, the evidence suggests, a widening of inequalities of access to education – and in consequence, the superior 'knowledge-jobs' it makes possible. This may or may not be helpful to the development of a 'successful knowledge economy'; it is certainly not helpful to the many who will be left on the sidelines of its development.

A further illustration of the dilemmas presented by the rise of the 'knowledge economy' is the proliferation of intellectual property rights that has been its legal correlate. As argued in Chapter 12, these are leading to an inegalitarian and exploitative form of globalisation that leaves many communities and societies unable to access the benefits of new knowledge. The accumulation and exploitation of such assets has become a central strategic focus not only for private corporations but also, increasingly, higher education institutions and other public research bodies. This trend represents a problematic extension of commodification and exclusionary claims into what was previously a public domain of scientific research and intellectual creation, which produced culture and knowledge as a non-exclusionary public or social good to be enjoyed and developed by all.

There is a tension between a knowledge economy and a knowledge society. Firms have a vested interest in enclosing knowledge in tight intellectual property rights, whilst it is in the interest of government and society to promote the widest possible intellectual commons. Such questions are posed particularly sharply by the rapid internationalisation of the intellectual property regime through TRIPs and the WTO, backed by the self-interests of already powerful countries; this now presents an almost insurmountable barrier to the development of knowledge-based economies, not to mention the eradication of preventable poor health and disease, in the global south.[52] Such a reckoning with the human and global consequences of commodifying and exploiting vital technological and scientific information should give pause to those who enthuse uncritically about knowledge-based economic strategies as the 'progressive' response to maintaining 'competitiveness' in a globalised world.

The value and promise of the knowledge economy, then, is not the contribution it can make to maintaining positions of relative economic privilege, but to advancing social goals and improving the quality of life. We need to look carefully at, and think creatively about, the ways in which knowledge-production is funded and incentivised, how access to knowledge is regulated, and how its benefits are distributed, both at home and abroad. If, as was argued above, the knowledge economy is more dependent than has hitherto been recognised upon collective action and public support, we need not only to strengthen and develop these dimensions, but also ensure that it truly serves the public interest. This of course opens up a range of difficult and complex questions, and work on alternative policy approaches – from 'open source' software and 'creative commons' licensing to introducing greater public participation in the development of science – has barely begun. But it represents an exciting and vital new agenda for a progressive political economy, which can lead to real economic dynamism and prosperity.

6 The value of the care economy

A political economy concerned with promoting well-being, social justice and environmental sustainability must think about the economy of care, which is something that has been overlooked by traditional economists. A good society needs to ensure that all its citizens receive good quality care, without unfairly burdening those who provide that care. Since women are the vast majority of carers in both the unpaid and paid economies, this is an issue that has important gender implications. Carers UK has estimated that unpaid caring in the UK would cost £57 billion if it were paid, and this of course does not indicate the value of care to the economy, which is much higher due to its contribution to the well-being, social capital, education, health and longevity of citizens. In other words, many of the things that the formal economy depends upon for success come from the underpinnings of the care economy. We need to understand the value of the care economy, how it underpins the formal economy and what we can to do preserve and strengthen it. Our neglect of the care economy has the logic of the farmer who killed his goose to get hold of the golden eggs inside. Our economic prosperity comes from the prosperity of the care economy.

This topic was explored in some detail in *The Good Society*, which recommended free child and social care, a better trained care workforce and valuing care through a participation income. This chapter complements the approach taken in that volume.

UK governments have tended to see the provision of care as a private responsibility, with the state as provider or funder of last resort. This is not how it is seen in some other European countries, particularly in Scandinavia, where ensuring that all who need it have a right to receive good quality care is seen as an aspect of social solidarity and a fundamental way to promote gender equality. A progressive government that adopted such a view of care and saw itself as sharing the responsibility of providing care with families could not only vastly improve the conditions under which adults and children are cared for, but could make a significant contribution to promoting gender equality in the UK.

The only viable way to ensure care of sufficient quantity and quality without unfairly disadvantaging carers is to work towards an economy based on a model of worker/carer citizens, in which all members of society have opportunities to contribute to both caring and paid employment, backed up by good quality public provision of care.

Caring has suffered from underinvestment for many years. All caring has a cost, even if that cost is a hidden one, paid for by the people who care unpaid for others and by those working in the paid economy whose skills are undervalued. The under funding of care results from a distortion that is effectively a subsidy by the poorest and weakest in society, and those who care for them, to those who are better able to look after themselves. That is something a progressive government should not tolerate and must make it a high priority to rectify.

Caring and employment

Caring, whether for adults or children, has significant effects on the employment situation of many women, and for a substantial minority of men. Others do not enter employment because of their caring or parental responsibilities. Policies that enable parents and carers to stay in employment while providing care would encourage and facilitate women's attachment to the labour market and, by enabling men to combine paid employment with unpaid care, help redress the imbalance between women's and men's contribution to caring and their unequal positions in the labour market.

There are two basic approaches to tackling the labour market disadvantages that parents and carers face: first to ensure that general conditions of employment are compatible with people making a substantial contribution to the care of children and adults, and second to allow for particular forms of leave that enable employees to devote more time to caring at particularly critical times. These two approaches are not incompatible. Even if we lived in a society which recognised citizens as worker/carers and with good caring services, there would be times at which a greater than normal input into caring would be required. However, the latter types of measures can lead to those who have to make use of them suffering other disadvantages, such as lower pay or discrimination. The correct balance of those two types of measures has to be judged carefully if they are to ameliorate rather than worsen gender inequalities, especially given the way that gendered caring norms mean that men and women are likely to react differently to these possibilities.

General conditions of employment

Ensuring that the general conditions of employment are such that they are compatible with making a substantial contribution to the care of children and adults requires reform of the labour market. In particular, people need to be able to work hours that are compatible with sharing caring responsibilities. This requires a change to the long working hours culture in the UK and a wholehearted implementation of the European Working-Time Directive.

The long working hours worked by men and by full-time women workers in the UK provide one of the main stumbling blocks to promoting great equality between fathers and mothers in both caring responsibilities and labour market opportunities. Many women are restricted to low paid part-time paid work because of the long hours that their partners work. This restricts both the father's ability to take part in caring for their child and the mother's available time for employment and her ability to take up labour market opportunities. As already noted, the UK's full-time hours for both men and women are – other than Latvia – the longest in Europe, and one in three fathers works more than 48 hours a week.

This is at least in part because the UK allows individuals to opt-out from the European Working Time Directive. However, decisions about the care of children and adults are not individual ones. Giving individuals who share caring responsibilities the choice about their working hours restricts the choices of their partners. Leaving aside the issue of whether all individuals who opt to work longer hours are really choosing to do so, it is important to recognise that, in practice, this is a right exercised by men at the expense of women's labour market opportunities. In order to promote more gender equality in both caring responsibilities and the labour market, and to give children better opportunities to be cared for by both parents, the UK government should give up its support for an individual opt-out to the Working Time Directive.

A further measure that could be adopted to ensure conditions of employment that are compatible with caring responsibilities is to give all workers the right to request a change in working hours in order to work flexibly. Currently this right to request is available only to parents of children under six. It is shortly to be extended to carers of adults but would more effective if it were extended to all workers. If the right to request flexible working were available to all workers, then employers would develop the capacity to respond to requests to work flexibly, and benefit from the better workplace culture that would result. This would in practice be more workable than the current need to make a special provision only for some employees. This change in culture could be speeded up by a tightening of the conditions under which a request can be refused. Further, if the right to request flexible working were extended to all, parents and carers would be in the same labour market position as other employees. This would remove any potential workplace resentment from other employees about 'special privileges', and ensure that parents and carers did not have to pay for those privileges in inferior pay or working conditions in other respects.

However, current regulations that surround the right to request flexible working are themselves too inflexible to meet the needs of parents, and in particular carers of adults. Changes in working hours through a right to request flexible working should not have to be permanent, so that parents and carers become trapped on reduced hours. One of the reasons why even short periods of part-time employment depress life-time earnings and opportunities in the UK is because women who take part-time jobs find it difficult to return to full-time employment.[53] Carers currently are less likely to return to the hours of work held prior to taking on caring responsibilities and this has a negative effect on their pension entitlements.[54] The current rules on the right to request flexible working reinforce this trap.

This is particularly important for carers of adults for whom future demands on their time are particularly unpredictable. A parent of a baby may not wish to change their working hours again until the child goes to school; although they should have the right to review their hours at regular intervals. But other carers may require more flexible arrangements than that. Requiring them to make a permanent change because they take on unpredictable caring responsibilities, lasting perhaps just a few months, will do nothing to rectify their labour market disadvantage.

There is a connection between the UK's long working hours and the right to request flexible working. Unless the political and workplace culture is seen to be supportive, carers will not take advantage of the right to request flexible working and the policy will not achieve its aims. The greater the difference in hours between those in full-time employment and those working 'flexibly', the more likely the latter will be penalised in terms of pay, career development and promotion. This is another reason why the government should not continue to insist on retaining the individual opt-out to the EU Working Time Directive, and should implement the Directive itself with more enthusiasm.

Leave for caring

Current statutory rights include some paid maternity and adoption leave, considerably less paid paternity leave, unpaid parental leave and 'reasonable' unpaid emergency leave, for example to help dependants if normal caring arrangements break down. Except for the last of these, there is no comparable leave for the carers of adults, nor for the care of children by anyone other than their biological or adoptive parents. Demographic changes mean that this is increasingly important as people have older parents and fewer siblings.

The length of leave that is needed for parents and carers partly depends on the availability of other forms of care. Currently, childcare provision for under threes is sparse in many parts of the country, leaving an inevitable gap which cannot be filled by the one year paid and unpaid maternity leave to which mothers are entitled, and the two lots of three months unpaid parental leave to which each of two parents are entitled (leaving aside the issue of whether taking the unpaid leave is affordable, particularly for a father).

One way to think of leave for caring is as a way in which the state can provide care. But like other forms of state provision it should be properly paid and not discriminatory in its regulations or its impact. Current forms of maternity, paternity and parental leave are discriminatory – only gender specific and unequal maternity and paternity leave is paid, and it is paid at a rate that would be too low for many families to afford to have their main earner take it. By European and rest of the industrialised world standards, UK maternity leave is already long. However, most other countries have longer periods of parental leave. There is no reason why women in the UK should face the possibility of being discriminated against by employers for in theory having long periods of maternity leave, while in practice they take no more time off than their European counterparts.

The government should take a lead in promoting a more egalitarian culture with respect to parental responsibilities. A change to 'parental' leave would only be effective in doing this if paid at a rate high enough for men to afford to take it. It should be an individual right (with an additional allowance for lone parents), so that fathers would have to take it or lose it. The total leave available to parent(s) should be of sufficient length to cover the gap between birth and the age at which a child would have an enforceable right to a high quality affordable childcare place.

It is also important that paid leave policies are developed for carers. The current right to emergency leave is useful for carers of adults, who may very suddenly have to take time off employment because of the unpredictability of the needs of the people they care for. However, such leave is only meant to be taken for a few days at a time and is anyway unpaid. As a complement to a better paid Carer's Allowance, largely for carers not in employment, eligible carers who do not claim it should be entitled to a certain number of paid days leave from employment per year. Leave should not be restricted to carers who are co-resident with or relatives of the recipient of care, and should be available proportionately to those who are caring less intensively than the 35 hours per week that entitle them to state support. The arguments given above for paying parental leave also apply to such carer's leave, where again it is particularly important to encourage take-up by male carers.

The care workforce

Ministers recognise that care is only as good as the people providing it,[55] but so far have failed to secure the resources required to develop and sustain a well rewarded, skilled and highly motivated care workforce. This task has been made harder because childcare and social care is now found mainly in the private for-profit sector. Over the last twenty years, in the name of increasing 'consumer choice' and achieving better value for money, local authorities have been obliged to transfer home care and residential care services for adults to the private for-profit sector. For similar reasons, most of the increase in childcare services since 1997, especially for pre-school children, has taken place in this sector. Experience shows that systems for holding private care providers to account are not well developed compared with those to which local authorities must conform.

The consequences of this shift have been bad for care workers as well as for those who need their services. The care workforce has never been well paid in the UK, but as local authority workers they had reasonable conditions and some opportunities for training. Turnover rates were low and levels of job satisfaction high because they had time to develop relationships with their clients. In the for-profit sector, pay and conditions are lower. After all, most of the cost of providing care is accounted for by care workers' wages and in order to keep profits high enough to attract and keep investors, there are inevitably strong pressures to keep wages down. As a result turnover rates have increased, doubling in many cases. Faced with recruitment difficulties in some areas, private providers turn to migrant workers, and if they are undocumented the opportunities for exploitation are considerable.

Care provided in these circumstances is likely to be poor. Good and safe care takes place within a relationship based on trust and familiarity. This takes time to develop and is not likely to be achieved if care is delivered by numerous care workers delivering 'packages' of care of no more than 15 minutes each. England is different from most EU countries in becoming so reliant on the market to provide care. There is no evidence that this care is either better or cheaper for those who need it. Leaving social goods such as the provision of care to the private market risks altering the very nature of those goods.

The increased economic activity rates of mothers and older women must not be achieved by exploiting those who provide the essential substitute care. It is important to reduce inequalities between women as well as between men and women. However, this is not to argue either that care is best left to families or that carers within the family should never be paid, for fear of undermining their motivation to care, as some argue.[56] The introduction of some free personal care for dependent adults in Scotland shows that formal care and family care are not interchangeable in a simple way, and that provision of such care does not reduce the willingness of families to care.

Changing the economy that we have today towards an economy that meets the needs of caring for society would have a transformative effect in improving the quality of life of everyone in society and restoring the underpinnings of the formal economy. We cannot have a dynamic and innovative economy without a strong care economy. At its heart a new political economy must move from the work ethic to the care ethic.

7 The quality of working life

A political economy based on well-being, social justice and environmental sustainability must deal with the issue of working life, and in particular the question of good work. Work consumes much of our adult lives. It is one of the places where we find satisfaction, friendship and even romance. Yet while many of us would agree that we should work to live rather than live to work, nobody is indifferent about their experience of employment. How we work, when and where we work and how long we work determines our over-all quality of life and can affect our general health and even our life expectancy. Yet despite its recognised importance, the quality of work as experienced by the majority has not featured on the political agenda for some considerable time. This is a genuine surprise, not least because a political party that can speak directly to the experience of most workers might expect to be rewarded with a substantial electoral dividend.

We know that in the 'hourglass' labour market we have more 'good' (high wage and high skill) jobs in the UK than at any time in the recent past, but we also have more 'bad' jobs too.[57] The Work Foundation cites persuasive evidence that 'the quality of working life has fallen over the last decade. Employees report less satisfaction with working hours, difficulties in reconciling work and their caring responsibilities – despite the present government's 'family friendly' policies – fewer opportunities to influence their working environment, more stress and more pressure'.[58] Job tenures are in fact relatively stable, but the accelerating pace of change within organisations, and increasing pressure to adapt to survive, mean that perceived insecurity is high, with one in six British workers saying they are uncertain about the future of their jobs.[59]

The government has taken some measures to improve working lives and move towards a more regulated labour market. The National Minimum Wage, social chapter rights, extended parental leave and rights to request flexible working, union recognition procedures, and tighter dismissal rules, are significant achievements (and tax credits have led to some redistribution, although they have also sometimes propped up poor quality jobs). It may be too early to assess the impact of these changes, but initial findings from the latest Workforce Employment Relations Survey suggest that they have yet to effect a qualitative transformation of our working experiences – since 1998 the availability of flexible working has improved but employees do not seem to perceive a significant change; employees' sense of achievement at work has improved but satisfaction with pay or influence has not; the incidence of 'high commitment' or 'high involvement' workplaces has not improved; and there has been a continuing 'decline in representative forms of employee voice'.[60] Moreover, it is hard to detect a well-articulated conception of what constitutes 'good work' from this diverse portfolio of policies. This should be regarded as an exciting opportunity for government, and in the present climate a re-politicisation of workplace issues could move the national policy debate on from the current obsessive focus on issues of crime and national security and the performance of tax-funded public services.

A vision of good work

There are a number of things that might constitute a vision of good work. One aspect is full employment – defined as the availability of paid work for all those who want it. It also includes fair pay and the absence of discrimination on the grounds of race, gender, class, sexuality, disability or age. But there are also a range of issues which go beyond contractual working conditions. A quality of work agenda is about secure and interesting jobs that employees find fulfilling, and work which enables people to develop and apply their skills. It implies greater levels of choice, flexibility and control for workers over working hours, rights to paid leave for specific family and caring responsibilities and more autonomy and control over the pace of work and the working environment. Workplace democracy is also crucial – there needs to be voice for workers in the critical employer decisions that affect their futures. The agenda is also concerned with work which meets the real human needs of consumers, and with environmentally sustainable workplaces where unions and employees are able to contribute to greening the workplace

This chapter considers the situation in relation to paid employment, and makes some suggestions for how progress could be made. But there is more to working life than paid work. Unpaid work, for example in the form of volunteering, and the provision of care in the household, is also central to our lives. These issues are tackled across all three volumes in the Programme for Renewal, including in the previous chapter.

Rethinking 'flexibility'

The neo-liberal approach to 'structural reform' and the need for flexible labour markets is epitomised by the *Jobs Study* published by the OECD in 1994.[61] Simply put, the argument runs that a Keynesian style reflation will have no impact on unemployment because of 'structural weaknesses' in the economy – inflexible labour markets, over mighty trade unions, inappropriate minimum wages and so on. An increase in effective demand therefore leads inevitably to higher inflation unless action is taken to remove rigidities and improve performance on the supply side. In practical terms the *Jobs Study* narrative has been associated with a number of views: that wage flexibility is essential, and that trade unions should therefore be weak and collective bargaining should be decentralised; that minimum wages should be kept low and young people should be paid lower rates or excluded completely; that strong employment protection laws lead to increased unemployment – hence the argument for labour market deregulation; that unemployment benefits should be kept low, durations should be limited, and job search requirements should be stringent; and that active labour market programmes must be developed to equip the excluded with the skills they need to return to work.

With the exception of the last point, it is reasonable to say the OECD's story could be read as an endorsement of the US model. It has exercised a powerful influence on debates around the European 'social model', informing the development of the 'Lisbon Agenda' and furnishing justification for the retrenchments of labour market regulation and social protection currently underway in France and Germany. The UK Labour government has been an ardent advocate of 'flexibility', laying particular stress on the 'social exclusion' argument that employment 'rigidities' may have the particular effect of restricting opportunities for marginal groups such as the young, the old, recent immigrants or women returning to work after childcare. As we have seen, there have been some moves towards re-regulation since 1997, but the UK workforce remains one of the least protected in the advanced industrial world, a position that the government seems highly reluctant to surrender.[62]

But the assumption that an Anglo-American model of 'labour flexibility' is the necessary condition of full employment in today's world is a dangerous myth that is not borne out by the evidence. A recent review of international data over the past two decades concluded that 'marginal workers in the "flexible" United States and United Kingdom fare no better, and frequently far worse, than their counterparts in the rest of the OECD'; that 'rising nonparticipation accounts for all of the improvement in aggregate unemployment'; and that 'much circumstantial evidence supports the centrality of macroeconomics in the success of both economies in the 1990s'. The 'systematic nature' of these results 'raises serious questions about the usefulness of OECD-IMF notions of flexibility as a basis for economic policy'.[63] By contrast, as the Work Foundation has argued, the 'strong employment performance' and 'labour market dynamism' of countries such as Denmark, Sweden, Austria and the Netherlands suggest that there may be much for the UK to learn from other EU member states.[64]

The OECD has itself recently reviewed its work and produced a more complex picture of what drives good labour market performance.[65] It concludes that wage flexibility remains important, but strong unions and co-ordinated collective bargaining are compatible with wage flexibility. Minimum wages fixed sensibly are compatible with good employment performance – the UK has had a rising minimum wage since 1999 with no adverse impact on employment. The impact of employment protection legislation on unemployment is 'small or ambiguous'. The level of benefits is much less important than the way in which they are administered – in other words it is possible to have high benefits, limited durations and rigorous job search requirements. Thus, far from being an endorsement of the US model, the OECD now sings the praises of the Danish system of 'flexicurity', which combines employment protection legislation (EPL) that is relatively low by international standards (though, it should be stressed, still considerably stronger than that in the UK) with high benefits, active labour market programmes, and some of the strongest trade unions in the world. Danish workers express a higher level of employment security than their British counterparts, despite somewhat shorter job tenures.

But, as one of the Labour government's own former members has argued, even 'employability for life' can be a poor substitute for long-term employment if it means a reduction in living standards, financial security, and trade union support.[66] In addition to learning how labour mobility might be facilitated and enhanced by high levels of unemployment benefit and strong trade union representation, we also need to recognise the ways in which job security and strong employment protection can themselves contribute to economic dynamism, by incentivising firms to invest in technological innovation and workforce re-training to meet changing patterns of demand. It is also likely that employees would tend to make a more positive contribution to innovation and productivity enhancement if they felt assured that their jobs would not be at risk as a result.[67] There may even be circumstances in which there is a trade-off between 'numerical flexibility' – the ease with which companies can 'hire and fire' – and 'functional flexibility' – the ease with which workers are able to undertake new tasks. Thus it has been suggested that the supposed 'rigidities' in Germany's systems of wage determination, employment protection, and workplace representation have played a crucial role in maintaining productivity growth and keeping the economy on a high investment, high skill, high-value-added growth path.[68] Similarly the National Institute of Economic and Social Research has suggested in relation to Britain's 'productivity gap' that 'successful productivity performance requires a stable institutional framework for long-term investments in human and physical capital, which the European model has been particularly good at providing over the last half century'.[69] At present there are particular concerns that our manufacturing base is not being developed because multinational firms are more likely to commit major investments in production and workforce development on the continent where employment protection is stronger.[70]

Any intelligent engagement with the economic evidence and with the real conditions of wealth creation, then, suggests a compelling case for moving decisively towards a 'positive model of flexibility' which combines high levels of employment opportunity, high levels of workplace productivity, and a fair distribution of the benefits and burdens of economic change.[71] A progressive political economy must be based upon a conception of flexibility that truly liberates and empowers, rather than subjecting the majority to the short-term dictates and irrational volatilities of the marketplace.

Promoting good work

For most people the quality of working life has dropped, even if pay has risen. Progress demands rather more than just a new initiative to establish more employment rights. Minimum standards are essential, but it is impossible to legislate high quality jobs into existence, require that all workers trust their employers or guarantee that all managers are able to make the best use of a highly skilled, well-motivated workforce. The correct policy mix will combine some regulatory intervention with a degree of exhortation, but government must also take responsibility for the identification, dissemination and application of best practice. Trade unions also have a crucial role to play. Research suggests there is a strong correlation between people having a trade union voice in the workplace and feeling they are treated fairly at work and have control of their working environment.[72]

The hourglass economy means that those with 'lovely' jobs face some different challenges to those with 'lousy' jobs. People at the top of the hourglass tend to have good terms and conditions and pay. Their primary interests are in greater control and flexibility, training and development and career progression. As is explored in *Democracy and the Public Realm* trade unions need to evolve to meet the needs to workers at the top of the hourglass as well as focusing on traditional issues such as pay and working conditions which are relevant to those at the bottom. We should explore measures to give people more control over their working lives – the issue of workplace democracy is also explored in *Democracy and the Public Realm*. We need more research into what brings well-being at work. Happiness research is a relatively new field and will continue to provide insights as it grows. There are already useful insights from the work on 'flow', which suggests that we gain satisfaction in our work to the extent that it is challenging but at a level at which we have the skills to meet that challenge.[73]

At the bottom of the hourglass, people – women, ethnic minorities and exploited migrants – work for low pay, often in poor conditions and with insecure jobs. Discrimination is still rife – for example women from certain ethnic minorities are three times as likely to be asked about their plans for marriage or children as white women.[74] A knowledge economy based on high skills and high wages will not help those at the bottom of the hour glass. Here the priority is to have a better deal in terms of pay and employment protection. The government must take forward its commitment from the Warwick Agreement to developing good employment standards. Other mechanisms to do this might include cracking down on the gender pay gap through compulsory equal pay audits, extending standards to the private sector through fair wages resolutions, and some of the measures explored in *The Good Society*, such as paying a living wage in the public sector, reasserting the role of the public sector as 'model employer', and using procurement to drive up employment standards.[75] We should also consider extending employment legislation to the small firms that constitute 85 per cent of British employers – a point discussed in more detail in chapter 9.

We need a different approach to the informal economy, which is large – around 7 per cent of GDP – and sits between the private economy and the household economy. Punitive measures to tackle informal work have limited success where poverty is the major driver. Research shows that much informal working is due to low benefit rates, low wages and disincentives to returning to formal work such as the loss of related benefits.[76] The welfare and tax system should gain a better understanding of why people work informally and should provide greater support for people who wish to make the transition to formal work.

There are also two further issues considered in *The Good Society* that are of relevance here. First, we need to deal with the issue of long working hours. This is not a middle-class issue – it is mainly male manual workers who are compelled to work more than 48 hours a week in order to supplement their low wages with overtime.[77] Secondly, we need to stop scapegoating migrant workers. They are not causing unemployment and they are net contributors to the economy. We must tackle employers who pay migrants below the minimum wage and landlords who give them sub-standard accommodation. We should deal directly with localised problems where there are pressures on public services, rather than arguing for ending migration.

Skills, learning, and self-development at work

Raising workforce skills through vocational training and lifelong learning offers a key route to increasing economic prosperity at the same time as improving the quality of people's working lives and turning them into a means of empowerment and self-development.

This has been identified as a particular challenge for the UK, where employees have been poorly served by existing systems of education and workplace training in comparison with other countries. Today 7 million adults lack basic skills in literacy, numeracy and the use of information and communication technology. Around a third of adults do not hold the equivalent of a basic school-leaving qualification. Too many young people cease education and training at age 16, and not enough are completing vocational or academic degrees. On all these dimensions the UK lags far behind comparable economies in Europe, North America and Asia. Moreover, from a social justice point of view, the distribution of skills and qualifications across the UK workforce is highly uneven and unequal, exacerbating the 'hourglass' polarisation of incomes and working lives, and reinforcing concentrations of poverty and exclusion in disadvantaged districts and regions.

The Labour government has pushed these issues up the policy agenda and has developed a raft of interventions and targets to begin to redress these problems. Most obviously, there has been increased investment in pre-school, primary and secondary education. But there is also recognition that, for the majority of today's workforce, improvements in the initial education system are now too late, and new opportunities for adult learning and re-skilling have been created, with initiatives such as the expanding enrolment in Modern Apprenticeships; 'Level 2' entitlement offering free tuition to those most seriously failed by the education system; and the National Employer Training Programme (now rolling out nationally as 'Train to Gain') to encourage employer engagement with the learning agenda.

Further action will be needed if we are to wrench the UK economy out of its longstanding 'low-skills equilibrium'. The Treasury-commissioned Leitch review, due to offer its final report later this year, has already noted that, while 'delivering current ambitions will improve the UK's skills and qualifications profile and lead to significant economic and social benefits', 'further improvements and a higher ambition are likely to be needed to meet the challenge of global change'. In particular, it has noted that, despite the high-profile emphasis on expanding higher education, additional investment in 'low' and 'intermediate' skills may offer the most cost-effective way of deriving economic benefits through increased employment and productivity, at the same time as having a greater impact in reducing income inequalities and regional disparities.

It is important here to emphasise that the key to moving the UK economy onto a 'high-skills' trajectory will be an increase in the demand for skills from employers, not simply the supply.[78] The Leitch review has noted that an increased supply of skilled workers will not be effectively used unless 'businesses ... adjust their strategies to adapt to this'. Unless firms upgrade their product market strategies, service standards, work organisation and job design, upskilling the workforce may result only in over-qualification and under-utilisation.[79] This means radical and proactive strategies to support the development of an expanding knowledge economy, as was outlined in chapter 5.

There may also be a need to strengthen the rights of employees to seek and access ways of developing their skills and capacities, and for a tougher line on employers who fail to offer meaningful opportunities to do so. The government has recognised that skills are a classic area of 'market failure' – individual employers may seek to 'free-ride' on training and experience provided elsewhere – and on this basis has sought to offer inducements to employers to allow their workers time off to gain new skills and qualifications. But take-up has been patchy, and it has recently been reported that, despite government incentives and subsidies, it is still the case today that more than one in three workers have been offered no training of any kind by their employers over the past year.[80] The TUC has persuasively argued that the government must be ready to develop a 'post-voluntary' framework for workforce development where the 'soft-touch' has failed to produce results – including a legal right to paid time off to train for all workers lacking level 2 qualifications, and the introduction of statutory training levies in sectors where employers are failing to meet the needs of their workforces.

These limitations on the progress achieved so far point to the shortcomings of the government's proclaimed 'employer-led' approach to skills and learning, and the need to move further in the direction of an 'employee-led' strategy. For while employers will certainly benefit from a better skilled workforce, we cannot rely entirely on their enlightened self-interest to deliver it, nor should we allow this to define the skills agenda in a way that restricts its wider economic and social potential. Evidence shows that even where employers do offer learning opportunities, these are concentrated in areas that offer short-term business advantage and often serve to reinforce rather than correct for existing inequalities in the distribution of skills across the workforce. On the other hand, the best progress in advancing a progressive skills agenda that can disseminate its benefits throughout society has been achieved through the efforts of trade unions acting to advance the wider interests of their members. Higher levels of workplace training are found in areas of high trade union membership, where more progress has been made in negotiating training agreements with employers. And one of the trade union movement's biggest recent success stories has been the development of a nationwide network of Union Learning Representatives who can help employees find and access new learning opportunities – which the government, to its credit, has supported, through the Union Learning Fund.[81] A logical next step would be to build on this success by incorporating training within the collective bargaining agenda covered by statutory recognition procedures, bringing the UK closer to the model of collectively-negotiated workforce development that has been so successful in other European countries and accounts for a large part of their skills advantage.

Ultimately, allowing employees to play an active and directing role in their own learning and development offers the best means to avoid the dangers of reducing or subordinating all learning and personal development to meeting the demands of the market. A truly progressive skills agenda would be one that used the workplace as a site for the development of productive powers and democratic capacities whose purpose and potential go beyond the requirements short-term employability.[82] A simple but emblematic illustration of this approach is provided by the TUC's recent call for the establishment of more workplace Book Clubs or 'borrowing shelves' – currently found in only a quarter of workplaces – which could facilitate improvements in literacy and encourage new forms of participation and engagement.[83] The 'skills agenda' should thus be embraced and extended, but also radicalised and democratised, so that it can provide the means not only to 'good work' but also to good life and a good society.

Transport for employment

The Social Exclusion Unit in its report *Making the Connections*, found that lack of transport is a barrier to work for two out of five jobseekers. The cost of transport is prohibitive for a quarter of jobseekers. Good quality access to the labour market through high quality transport is essential to ensure access to employment opportunities. Public spending on buses is less than half the spending on railways, yet two out of three public transport journeys are made by bus. Privatisation of buses has produced a market failure in the provision of accessible and affordable public transport to employment hubs. Flexible 24/7 work patterns exacerbate this problem and advantage those with cars, and men over women. Transport planning and resourcing should enable those people marginalised in the job market to access opportunities. There should be a new regulatory structure which includes subsidies and duties that recognise the role of transport for disadvantaged residents in access to employment. As discussed in the next chapter, such infrastructure improvements could be funded by a land value tax, which takes account of the increase in land value as a result of the infrastructure.

There is a vicious circle where poor public transport means that employees prefer to drive and thus employers seek sites with good car parking, which tend to be out of town. This then makes journey patterns even more fragmented, which makes it even harder for the public transport system to be viable. As argued in chapter 4, we should consider measures to make employers locate back into town centres, which would create high enough concentrations of jobs to support good radial bus services. This would help create a virtuous circle where people would be more keen to use public transport, and therefore more employers would want to locate at the bus node.

A Standing Commission

It is clear that an agenda around the quality of working life is extremely rich, and this chapter has only begun to sketch out some of the issues. In order to take this whole crucial area forward, government should create a Standing Commission on the Quality of Working Life. Modelled on the Low Pay Commission, it would involve employers, unions, government and others to come together with a shared social mission to consider the state of working life on an ongoing basis, and to recommend regulatory solutions and good practice through voluntarism. Such an institution would be symbol of our commitment to good work. Transforming the experience of people's working lives would lead to a new level of economic dynamism and innovation, putting us on the 'high road' to economic prosperity, as well as changing the quality of people's everyday lives.

8 Housing and land reform

C reating a democratic economy based on well-being, social justice and
environmental sustainability needs to deal with the issue of housing and
land. People's access to shelter and home life is fundamental to their well-being
and a matter of social justice. For people who own their home it is usually the
biggest asset they have. Poor housing is connected with a variety of other social
problems including bad health, crime and fuel poverty, and it creates local
tension, for example as seen in Barking and Dagenham, where the BNP use the
issue of housing as means of recruitment. Our homes are also a major source of
our environmental impacts. Thus housing and land is central to political economy.

Government's policy aim at present is that 'everyone should have the
opportunity of a decent home at a price they can afford, in a place in which they
want to live and work'.[84] But decent, affordable housing is increasingly
inaccessible for a growing percentage of the population. Whilst the value of
homes in the UK has risen 50-fold in the last 30 years, the distribution of housing
is highly unequal, with the wealthiest tenth of households possessing five times
the housing wealth of the tenth with the least wealth.[85] The high cost of housing
has a direct impact in creating homelessness, with more than 116,000 homeless
children living in temporary accommodation and more than 900,000 children
growing up in overcrowded conditions.[86] This is a truly shocking situation and
needs real systemic change.

The Barker Review of Housing Supply showed that there has been a massive
fall in housing production since the late 1970s, caused mainly by the end of
council house production by local authorities.[87] The result has been a chronic
undersupply, resulting in homelessness, overcrowding and a severe affordability
crisis. Most people in Britain now live in their own homes, and have acquired
huge asset wealth as house prices have soared, but an entire generation is now
largely excluded from the market.

There are two major criticisms of the current approach to housing policy. First,
policy is based on the assumptions that demand is fixed and that high house
prices are therefore a consequence of low supply. This analysis fails to appreciate
the special economic nature of housing and land assets, which renders
conventional market theories of supply and demand inadequate. It is not clear

that an increased supply will lead to more affordable homes, as the Barker Review assumes. The Review fails to confront the fact that the housing crisis has been hugely profitable for many ordinary homeowners, and that expectations of unearned and untaxed gains are a major driver of house prices themselves. Applying orthodox economic models to housing suggests that increasing land supply alone will solve the housing crisis. But there are serious problems with the demand side of the housing market and we need to take radical steps to solve them. Solving the affordability crisis requires a policy response based on a much broader look at the role of housing in the economy, especially the role of asset accumulation and land speculation in creating excess demand. These issues are dealt with below.

The second criticism of the current approach is that whilst housing growth is currently planned for the overheated and relatively overcrowded South East, at the same time the Housing Market Renewal Pathfinder programme is removing substantial housing from the north. Clearly there are problems of regional economic imbalance: housing and employment opportunities are not co-located. Thirty years ago the policy response would have been to focus on industrial development in the north: today the assumption is the jobs market cannot be influenced, and that therefore we have to deal with housing consequences. Reviving an interventionist approach to regional economic development, as suggested in chapter 10, could substantially reduce the need for housing growth.

Despite these caveats, it is clear that more housing does need to be built, and that the current policies and governance arrangements covering housing are failing to provide it. In the short term, improving the housing situation means public intervention and spending to increase the supply of new housing, especially social housing; enhancing the rights of private sector tenants; defending and enhancing the ability of public and non-profit agencies to provide affordable housing; creating a genuine intermediate sector; reducing housing market instability; and 'improving affordability' (reducing house prices relative to earnings.)

In the long term it means resolving fundamental problems in the supply of housing and land; more active regional policies to increase the demand for labour in the old industrial areas and away from the South East; managing the market to reverse regressive wealth distribution; reforming tenure to promote social equity; and doing all of this in a way that fits with the demands of an environmentally sustainable society. This chapter explores how we can take forward this longer term agenda.

Improving supply

Nearly a thousand years after the Domesday Book, only half of British land is registered. We do not know who owns most of the land in the country, although estimates suggest that a large proportion of it is held by a small landed aristocracy.[88] Land registration should be compulsory and the results freely available to all. A one year deadline should be set, after which all unregistered land would become public property.

Public subsidy should be aimed at providing permanently affordable homes, and the recent move towards subsidising demand for homeownership reversed. In the short term this means a massive programme of house building, on a par with the post-war council housing boom. The supply of affordable housing needs to increase dramatically. Private house building rates have stayed constant for decades, and commercial developers should not be relied on to significantly increase production. Public and non-profit agencies such as Registered Social Landlords, Urban Development Corporations and New Towns Corporations should be empowered to play a much bigger role in construction, including housing for the private market. If private and independent sectors do not deliver, the state should do so directly.

An important reason for the shortfall in housing supply is the decline of social provision. Private sector provision has remained fairly constant over recent decades but local authority housebuilding has dropped from highs above 300,000 a year in the 1950s and 1960s to the low hundreds today. The 'Right To Buy' policy has cut the stock of social housing by around half and continues to transfer tens of thousands of units a year into the private market. New build by Housing Associations – currently around 15,000 to 20,000 a year – is nothing like enough to make up the difference. Of all the crucial pillars of the welfare state it was social housing that suffered the most vicious cuts through the 1980s and 1990s. It requires a major programme of public investment and reforms to rebuild it, including giving local authorities full powers to finance investment by borrowing against their assets and revenue streams, just as Housing Associations are able to.

Mechanisms for long term land value capture should be used to fund major infrastructure projects. The most comprehensive of these is a land value tax (discussed further below), but others include property tax reforms, strategic use of public land ownership, and the use of public equity shares in new developments. It has been calculated that the Jubilee Line extension to Stratford has raised property values around the stations by £10 billion. If only a small part of this windfall had been taxed, it would have easily paid for the extension.

The emphasis on high density, mixed tenure, mixed use development in sustainable communities should be maintained. But actual planning delivery is in a state of near permanent crisis and needs reform and substantial new resources.

Managing the market

Booms and busts in the housing market are hugely damaging to the economy, social mobility and equality. The aim of public policy should be stable house price inflation, in line with earnings. Reducing regional imbalances in the housing market should be a priority for economic and employment policies.

There is nothing wrong with wishing to own our own homes: ownership brings legal, financial and psychological security, and encourages people to invest in upkeep and improvements. The problem is the expectation that home ownership will make us rich. It is fundamentally contrary to social equity that those who own homes are rewarded richly for the privilege of being housed, and that the better they are housed the better they are rewarded.

These unearned capital gains made by the owners of property are a natural site for taxation, especially given the increasing difficulty in taxing globally mobile capital. Locational benefits are land value gains, whereas improvements owners make to the actual building are reasonably theirs to keep. We should therefore shift the basis of property taxes off building value and onto land value, and off occupation and onto ownership. In the longer term the aim should be to replace all property taxes (Council Tax, Business Rates, Stamp Duty) with a full annual land value tax levied on all owners of landed property, based on the unimproved value of the site (i.e. ignoring buildings etc) but based upon the optimum rather than the actual use of the site.[89] This would mean that land owners would be given an incentive to develop their land as productively as possible.

Many countries use a land value tax, including Denmark, Singapore, Japan and Estonia. In Harrisburg, the capital of Pennsylvania, the impact of a land value tax has been profound on the local economy. It has played a key part in transforming the city from the second most run-down city in the US to a thriving local economy with the number of vacant sites cut by 85 per cent.

A land value tax would achieve many of the policy aims proposed here including stabilising the housing market, redistributing wealth inequalities, reducing tenure distinctions, reducing land speculation, promoting efficient use of land, reducing regional imbalances, rewarding improvements to buildings, ensuring development and regeneration benefits to local communities and funding public infrastructure.

We also need to change the incentives in relation to second homes, empty and underused properties. Full council tax for holiday homes should be mandatory, and local authorities allowed to apply higher rates for non-residents. Tax breaks for empty and derelict land and property should be abolished, and then reversed. This includes both Council Tax and Business Rates.

Reforming tenure

Successive governments have favoured owner occupiers and eroded the rights of private renters, and allowed social tenants to become residualised, resulting in massive redistribution in favour of the rich.[90] We must seek to minimise the inequality of life chances between different tenures, and to give people genuine tenure choices that enhance their mobility, security and quality of life. In particular, private tenants need greater protection and the reintroduction of rent controls.

A genuine intermediate sector is needed, providing realistic and attractive choices for people between the poles of debt-financed ownership and disenfranchised tenancy. Where intermediate owners benefit from subsidy, the public interest should be preserved in the form of equity shares. More permanent intermediate forms of tenure should be developed and promoted, including Community Land Trust (CLT) models of permanently affordable homeownership, which can preserve subsidy and share rising property values between occupiers and the rest of the community.[91] CLTs are based on the idea that natural resources are owned in common in trust for the benefit of present and future generations, rather than for the benefit of an individual property owner. They are run democratically on the basis of one member one vote.

A Community Right to Buy should be established, supported by national and regional loan funds, building on the successful elements of the Land Reform (Scotland) Act.[92] This would give communities the first refusal to acquire property assets they have a reasonable interest in, including open spaces, woodland, local shops, community facilities and housing. Local authorities should be empowered to support the development of CLTs, and to safeguard local public assets CLTs should be put on a secure legal basis, ensuring that their assets cannot be carpet-bagged through demutualisation or leaseholder enfranchisement. There should be safeguards that they will involve excluded groups and will not erode staff conditions.

A policy of flexible equity would mean that people could buy into housing equity easily, at a low base, without the need to borrow vast sums. This would encourage saving and make home ownership in some form a realistic aspiration for everyone that wants it. Lots of older people live in poverty and yet have huge housing assets that they cannot access. Flexible equity also means developing socially responsible forms of equity release, enabling people to sell some of their housing equity. Enabling elderly homeowners to more easily release housing wealth benefits them, reduces welfare costs, and enables improvements in the housing stock.

Building regulations

Our homes are a major part of our environmental impact, so a transition to a more sustainable society demands we grapple with this. Green home standards should be enhanced and made mandatory, with hard targets for on-site generation of energy for new developments, and real consideration of the effects of climate change. However, the tendency to focus public efforts only on new buildings should be reversed: 99 per cent of the housing supply is in existing buildings, and far more effort and investment needs to go into retrofitting houses to be more energy efficient, healthy and secure. Energy companies should be encouraged to fund energy efficiency measures in homes, through smart metering and tax incentives, while incentives for homeowners should be enhanced.

Building regulations should require all new construction to be 'carbon neutral' over its lifetime: that is, to minimise energy use and greenhouse emissions in construction, use, maintenance and eventual demolition; to cover as large a proportion of emissions as possible through renewable energy production as part of the development package; and to offset any remaining emissions through accredited offsets at or before the time the emissions occur. Building regulations could require the best practicable energy efficiency measures to be installed whenever buildings undergo significant refurbishment. Grants financed from fuel taxes could be offered to cover the additional cost of fuel efficiency measures.

It is already possible to build new housing, and most other buildings, to produce no net carbon emissions, with known and proven technologies. The most effective techniques for reducing energy use are simple and well known, including built forms which minimise the external area to lose or gain heat, high levels of insulation in external surfaces, and layout to maximise use of natural light and capture solar heat. Energy efficient lights and appliances can further reduce consumption. More sophisticated (but still well known) technologies such as heat pumps, solar water heating, photovoltaics, combined heat and power (preferably powered by biomass including organic wastes or energy crops) can then provide for reduced energy needs. There is therefore no need to wait for more technologies.

Zero-energy performance typically adds only a few percentage points to construction costs, and costs are usually more than recouped in lower running costs over the lifetime of the building; and in any case additional construction costs are mostly absorbed in lower prices developers pay landowners for land. Therefore better energy performance would not impose additional costs on citizens wanting to buy homes, but could be funded largely out of reduced profits from land speculation.

Reforming our housing and land system so that it is environmentally sustainable and equitable is a crucial part of creating the good economy. Without this we will have a whole generation of people condemned to lead lives excluded from the housing market, a boom bust housing market that will threaten the rest of the economy, and homes that are major contributors to the problems of climate change.

9 Socialising the market

A political economy that is focused on well-being, social justice and environmental sustainability requires a boldness in actively shaping markets and market actors, rather than a passive response to what a deregulated market brings – which has been more characteristic of the UK approach. Shaping markets can create more innovation and prosperity than deregulated free-for-alls where the drive for short-term profit constrains investment and leads to exploitation of vulnerable workers and the environment. There are a number of areas where useful work can be done around market and corporate reform: a bolder approach to regulating markets, more work to support diverse enterprises, and new measures to civilise corporations.

Constructing better markets

Over the last two decades the argument about regulation has been defined in terms of liberty and efficiency. It has been popular to argue that regulation is authoritarian, violating the rights of individuals to go about their business without interference, and that bureaucrats in the public services cannot respond quickly or effectively to changing demand. But the pursuit of private profit does not always or automatically advance the public interest. Markets can be illiberal and inefficient and the private sector can engage in rent-seeking behaviour, and block innovation in order to lock-in markets. Therefore we need to test markets regularly, to see whether they provide consumers with value for money and appropriate goods and services; whether the providers are accountable; what the impact on wider stakeholders is; and how they contribute or detract from wider public policy goals. Appropriate architecture can build quality, functioning markets which meet people's needs.

We need to get better at constructing and shaping markets which demand high quality performance and social benefit from providers. This means we need a new conversation about what kinds of frameworks lead to good outcomes for all stakeholders: business, employees, local communities and so on. And government needs to be braver in arguing that regulation promotes high quality business and other social goods, and acts as a spur to innovation. We should take heed of best practice from around the world. For example on environmental issues we can look at the Irish plastic bags tax, or the German legislation on waste packaging – and we should also develop our own new regulations, such as creating goods which do not have wasteful standby switches.

Business recognises the need for rules and understands that many forms of regulation do not negatively affect business in the medium term. For example in June 2006 business leaders from a number of companies, including B&Q, Vodaphone and Shell, asked government to impose tougher climate change regulations, as this would be a spur for innovation and give British business an edge with new technology. Similarly, a DTI survey of a representative sample of small business showed that twice as many backed new employment rights as found them a burden. Business lobby organisations have overstated the case of the regulatory burden in the UK, through measures such as counting the cost of paying the minimum wage as a regulatory cost, or by describing measures which command widespread support such as the control of workplace asbestos as red tape.[93] The UK is in fact ranked by the OECD as the most liberal economy in the world on its composite indicator of flexibility.

We also need a new role for regulators. Regulators have by and large seen their role in narrow economic terms. They need to shift to meet new demands by taking a more active role in protecting the worst off, and at the same time moving to smarter regulation using a more systemic approach to managing complexity, rather than trying to use more and more detailed rules to try and manage unmanageable situations.[94] Regulators could be opened up to more democratic representation by workers and trade unions and other stakeholders as they are often extremely unaccountable – there is much to learn from the American model of regulatory commissions, which meet in public and enforce a greater transparency on regulated industries. Regulatory challenges are increasingly global. One mechanism to deal with this is to increase the strength of global regulatory networks by bringing together regulators from across the world to forge relationships and exchange learning.[95]

Whilst corporate social responsibility (CSR) is to be welcomed, it cannot replace the need for appropriate market frameworks and governance structures. Often the most responsible corporations are penalised, as other firms who do not meet such environmental or social standards may be able to provide a service at a cheaper cost. And CSR is often more focused upon public relations than on creating real change, and it is a hard job for the consumer to try and tell whether or not it is the real thing. Similarly whilst the role of ethical consumption is another important market led driver for change, its effect tends to be marginal and it is easy to manipulate.

Our frameworks need to protect the interests of the weakest. For example research shows that many of the UK's most deprived locations are becoming 'free

ATM deserts'.[96] The poorest and least mobile people, and rural communities in particular, are having to pay each time they withdraw money. Regulation for banks to provide free ATMs shows the sort of approach we need for markets to meet human needs based on universal service obligations.

We should consider strengthened competition and anti-monopolies policy, at local, national and international levels, to prevent large companies from using their financial muscle to unfairly drive others out of business. Established businesses dislike competition, but the government has sometimes missed this point, as it has confused the market with business lobbies and rich individuals. We need to make business lobbying far more transparent, and to promote proper functioning markets through appropriate competition legislation for any given market, and through ensuring the voices and interests of smaller businesses are heard.

Many markets need regulating for the public interest. Just one example is fund management in the City. The performance of highly paid City fund managers is woeful. Ordinary workers are expected to increase their productivity and performance in the face of the pressures of globalisation, but only one in eight fund managers consistently outperforms the benchmark FTSE All share index. Yet salaries for UK fund managers have not fallen – the median remuneration for UK fund managers is $217,000. Whilst the City is the champion of market forces, this is a market that is failing in its own terms. Although there is an oversupply of financial products in the market, prices have not fallen, and the whole industry is being cross-subsidised by our own individual pensions and savings. The drive for profit leads to a failure to meet real public needs. For example in 1990 the financial regulator found that of the 870,000 pensions sold by the Prudential, as many as nine out of ten were based on misleading or incorrect advice. Financial products need to be better regulated to actually create value for consumers.

Another area that is crucial in shaping markets is dealing with investor short-termism. Pension funds signal to fund managers that they are seeking short-term performance. This impacts on their investment decisions, and puts pressure on company managers to deliver short-term share price rises rather than longer term sustainable growth. This leads to market failures such as misallocated capital (e.g. the technology boom of the 1990s) and into short-term mergers and acquisitions activity which often does not deliver for shareholders or employees. It hinders industry from taking the longer term view that is needed to develop new technologies, invest in capital intensive industries and keep its workforce together when trading conditions are adverse. At its worst the pressure to make a fast buck can lead to corporate catastrophes such as Enron. There are a range of possible mechanisms to deal with short-termism.[97] Any solution will need to deal with investors, business, analysts, government and unions – a single intervention will not change the entire system. Example policies could include trustees implementing long-term mandates with fund managers, strengthened worker involvement in company decision-making, use of the 'precautionary principle' in relation to mergers and acquisitions, and a change in corporate governance principles (the Combined Code) to link executive pay with long-term shareholder value.

Supporting diverse enterprises

Small and medium sized enterprises (SMEs) are core to the economy but their particular needs are often overlooked. There are around 23 million SMEs in the EU, contributing 75 million jobs.[98] Most small businesses work in local markets, and act as the glue that holds their communities together through employment and social networks. They can play a crucial role in preserving the local in the era of the global economy. Small business is also a major source of innovation in the economy: 64 per cent of all commercial innovations in the UK come from SMEs. Many people are becoming entrepreneurs or setting up small businesses. Their motives are often in line with what a left political economy is based upon: not pure financial gain but a desire for independence and a higher quality of working life.

This needs to be balanced, however, by the fact that employment rights are weaker in small businesses – they often have the poorest working conditions and they do not have trade union recognition rights. We need a 'new deal' for small business. On the one hand this should extend employment protection and trade union rights to small firms. But this needs to be complemented with a government agenda that is more focused upon the needs of smaller business, and understands their role in providing employment, innovation and strengthening local communities, and their needs in terms of regulatory impact, support, training and finance. In particular we need to think much harder about how to promote learning in the SME economy.

The economy is more than just private businesses. *Democracy and the Public Realm* considers how we can support the wider third sector/civil society. Part of the third sector are organisations known as 'social enterprises' that access resources from markets and use it to create some form of positive social change such as the reduction of inequality. They include co-operatives and mutuals, fair-trade organisations and many other business models which are primarily driven by social or environmental purpose. According to figures from the Government's Annual Small Business Survey 2005, and existing data for the social enterprise sector, there are at least 55,000 social enterprises in the UK with a combined turnover of £27 billion per year. Social enterprises account for 5 per cent of all businesses with employees, and contribute £8.4 billion per year to the UK economy – almost 1 per cent of annual GDP. More work needs to be done to learn the lessons for social enterprise from existing models such as housing associations, social care and leisure trusts, especially around governance and accountability. There also needs to be much more work to spread social innovation: there are many examples of innovation but they tend to remain small-scale rather than achieving viral change. The achievements of those businesses that take a socially entrepreneurial approach should be publicised, to capture the imaginations of younger generations and future entrepreneurs about what is possible through value-driven organisations. More demanding regulatory regimes, as suggested earlier in the chapter, will provide quality social enterprises with a competitive advantage, whereas low-grade regulation or procurement of the cheapest product disadvantage good social enterprises that provide social and environmental added-value beyond their competitors.

The concept of social enterprise, however, should not be fetishised, and in particular we should not be wedded to the idea that particular legal forms have better impacts, or that all socially beneficial activity should take place within 'social' organisations. All business – small and large – should be encouraged to make positive social and environmental impacts. Legal forms should not be given a tax benefit or rebate on the basis that they are necessarily more 'socially positive'.

It is also important that the buzzword of social enterprise is not used as a smokescreen to roll back the welfare state or open up public services to private firms. This is a danger at the moment: for example health as a public service is being opened up to private provision. There are real concerns about whether the health services should be opened up to the market at all – they need to be properly integrated and universally orientated in ways that can be undermined by fragmentation and the introduction of competitive and commercial incentives. At the same time, the relative freedom of 'third sector' organisations from government direction can enable them to work flexibly and innovatively and develop closer relationships with their user communities. We need to think carefully and debate honestly about the costs and benefits of turning to independent providers for the provision of public services. Where there is a case for looking beyond the public sector, it is essential that enough work is done to create a supply base of small firm and social enterprise providers. Without this support and market-making it is likely that any public services opened to contestability will simply be swept up by a few large private firms, leading in the medium term to less choice and innovation and more cost – precisely the opposite of what was promised. We also need to ensure that measures are in place to make sure that independent providers are not cutting costs at the expense of the pay, working conditions or job security of their staff.

Civilising corporations

Whilst the New Labour government has taken measures to help lower paid workers, it has done far less in relation to the employers. Companies are part of society and need to be good citizens – they need to meet responsibilities along with the rights that we give them. In an era where we are calling for public services to be more accountable to citizens we also need companies to be accountable, and to enhance society and the environment rather than degrade them. Progress on this agenda since Labour came to power has been limited. New regulations representing a small advance in social and environmental reporting were introduced but then rapidly abolished to appease business and investor interests; and in its major reform of company law – the eight-year long Company Law Review – the government shied away from introducing a stakeholder or 'pluralist' approach to directors' duties, opting instead to maintain the duty to shareholders as the primary, overriding duty on company directors, while also ensuring that it is still the case that only shareholders who have the power to enforce directors' duties.

The contemporary company or corporate form is thoroughly out of date. It needs modernisation. In particular we need to rebalance the extent to which shareholders and corporate entities are given primacy under UK law – for example directors' primary duties are to shareholders and the corporation. We need citizens and consumers and employees to be given the same level of rights as shareholders and firms. The issue of workplace democracy and employee control is explored in more detail in *Democracy and the Public Realm*.

There are a wide range of measures that could help move towards creating civil corporations.[99] In particular, large companies ought to be required to be more fully transparent at the highest levels – Enron is what happens when we do not accept this. Private corporations can sometimes exercise as much or more power than governments. It should thus be possible for citizens to access information about company meetings, holdings, and practices, about the reasons for certain decisions, business lobbying practices and so on. Whilst the situation has been improving a little in relation to public companies, at present companies are permitted levels of secrecy that serve to obscure their activities from citizens and consumers. Naturally companies have a right to privacy and protection from other companies when it comes to sensitive information, but that right should not override the public interest in ensuring that their activities are not socially harmful. Stakeholders should be granted more rights to inspect and assess company activities, particularly when they are acting in the public sphere – e.g. delivering public services or PFI contracts. Independent public bodies could be given the right to access all corporate information in very sensitive instances.

Another mechanism to improve corporate accountability would be implementation of the proposals for company reporting which make large and medium sized companies report on social, employee, supplier and environmental issues.[100] They should also report on equality and diversity, which could include some form of pay audit. Company reporting would help shareholders better analyse risks and understand which companies behave responsibly, and enable campaigners and consumers to have greater levels of information. But company reporting is not a panacea – to be effective it must be coupled with regulations requiring directors to act on the information included in their reports and stronger rights of redress for stakeholders who are harmed when directors fail to do this. Doing this requires changing the protection that directors receive under limited liability laws, which were designed to protect investors not senior employees. It also needs to be complemented with a strengthening of the public interest tests under the Freedom of Information Act. For example, at present information on financial misselling scandals is being withheld from the public by the Financial Services Authority on the basis of commercial confidentiality.

Directors should be legally obliged to minimise any damage their company does to local communities and the environment, and people overseas who are harmed by the activities of a UK company should be able to take action against them in a UK court.

We might also consider mechanisms for encouraging pension funds to use their might to hold companies socially and environmentally accountable – some are already beginning to do so, especially the insurance companies who are seeing the costs of the problems. For example this could be done through a requirement to engage with investee companies on their ethical performance. But legal requirements are not enough – we need a greater culture of institutional shareholder activism. This should be combined with strengthening shareholder and employee power over boardroom pay, and making sure that payment for failure is no longer tolerated at the top. Executive pay continues to spiral upwards unjustifiably. In 2005 the pay of directors of FTSE 100 companies rose by 28 per cent to an average of £32,263 a week, in contrast to average earnings which rose at 3.7 per cent. Research shows clearly that the inflation in senior executive pay is not because there is a global marketplace: 86 per cent of UK FTSE 250 CEOs are UK nationals, many of whom have spent a long time in the firm in which they take the top job.[101] Nor has the extraordinary rise in corporate remuneration been as a result of superior business success or a rise in entrepreneurialism and risk-taking – there is no evidence that firms are performing better than firms did in the more egalitarian 1950s and 1960s. As suggested by the Work Foundation, remuneration committees could use the common law principle of mitigation to deal with the problem of rewarding for failure.

A new political economy

A new progressive political economy would regulate markets in the public interest, support a diverse range of enterprises and make sure that companies are democratised so that they take seriously all stakeholders, not just shareholders. This would lead to a different kind of economy that everybody had a stake in. It would reduce many of the social costs that presently government and society have to pick up – for example when markets exclude people, when the environment is over-exploited, when high quality businesses are undermined by unregulated and unethical competitors, or when shareholder pressure for a quick buck forces them to engage in practices that are not beneficial to the consumer or society – e.g. misselling financial products. Intelligent market architecture could tip the economy into a virtuous circle where innovation meets the needs of the public interest, where good businesses are not penalised by short-term investors or by crooked competitors, and where there are higher levels of transparency and trust between corporations and their stakeholders.

10 The monetary and fiscal framework

Labour's record of steady growth and relatively high employment has been strong on the surface. However in the past 10 years growth and employment have been sustained by a one-off public spending boom (unlikely to be repeated and predicated upon starvation of the public sector from the 1980s up to 2000); a worrying increase in private debt (compensating, perhaps, for Labour's reluctance to increase public debt); and, most crucially, a deregulated, low-paid, under-unionised services sector that has been mopping up unemployment. All these things are 'costs' of our growth and employment record which might have been rendered unnecessary if the Labour government had been more expansionist. There is thus a sense in which the price of our economic success has been the 'social recession' described in *A Good Society*.

Unemployment in the UK has been persistently lower than in the Eurozone, and has declined relatively faster since 1997. This has not, as argued by neo-liberals, been due to labour market flexibility but, because UK macroeconomic policy has in practice left some room to take a moderately expansionary stance. Gordon Brown's Golden Rule postulates that the current deficit should be in balance over the economic cycle. In the UK, the increase in public investment of 65 per cent in real terms from 1997-8 to 2004-5 helped to sustain demand without running foul of the Golden Rule.

The potential danger in the government's present approach to demand management is that it does not provide for appropriate action to deal with the threat of recession. If a slowdown in the growth of demand and output were to raise unemployment, we would be entirely dependent on the Monetary Policy Committee (MPC) cutting interest rates to stimulate demand, even though keeping down unemployment is not within their remit. Cuts in taxation or increases in public expenditure would not officially be on the agenda. Admittedly the Chancellor sets the inflation target and therefore could revise it, but this seems like an unlikely action.

The Treasury should make it clear that it would be prepared to take expansionary budgetary measures if there was a threat of recession, and it should amend the remit of the MPC to include the maintenance of a high level of employment, as is the case with the Federal Reserve. New machinery could be set up to involve the unions and employers' organisations in the formation of economic policy, as part of a generally more participatory approach to economic and industrial management. Care would need to be taken to make MPC decision making transparent.

The government's 'Sustainable Investment Rule', that total public sector net debt must not exceed 40 per cent of GDP, is too restrictive. Most OECD countries carry public debt way above this level, and even the EU's Maastricht Treaty requires only that it should not exceed 60 per cent of GDP. There is in addition a strong argument that it makes no economic sense to impose limits on public debt without regard to the capital assets owned by the government, or to whether any of those assets yield additional revenue for the government (as would be the case with rail infrastructure and rolling stock).[102] This may not seem especially pressing at a time when public sector net debt stands at around 34.5 per cent of GDP and is projected to peak at 37.1 per cent of GDP in 2009-10. But the government's concern to keep public debt at a low level has been seen by many as an important driver behind the Private Finance Initiative and other dubious policies aimed at keeping publicly financed investment 'off the books'. We should consider ways of improving the design of the 'Sustainable Investment Rule' to reflect these concerns. We can also rethink our conception of investment as discussed in chapter 3. We should find new ways of mapping the costs and benefits of intergenerational transfers such as PFI or environmental resource use. We could create 'intergenerational accounts' which show the benefits gained now at a projected future cost and the justifications behind such decisions.

Taxation for a fairer society

Some public goods can be secured through regulation of markets; others need direct public provision. By and large, this means funding through taxation. On the one hand taxation reduces the disposable income available to an individual for consumption (although in most circumstances, it merely slows the rate at which individual private income grows). But if it provides for improved public goods – for lower crime, better schools, better public transport, better health care – it can increase the quality of the individual's life. Taxes are not a necessary evil, but a positive good, a contribution we each make both to our own well-being and to the common good. They provide the funding for the infrastructure which drives the economy forward. Taxation can make us better off and allows for the investment in those public goods, such as health, education and transport, that our future prosperity is based upon. We should, therefore, raise taxes over time to fund more public goods.

There is a myth that we must keep the tax burden as a share of national income below some 'magic figure' (currently 42 per cent) or else economic ruin will result. This is just not true – we have choices about our level of taxation and public good provision, and higher levels are not necessarily damaging our economic performance, even in very traditional economic terms. For example Sweden has high levels of productivity and economic growth (and is ranked number 3 in the World Economic Forum competitiveness report), with tax levels at around 51 per cent of GDP, as compared to just over 40 per cent in the UK.[103] As Adair Turner has said, levels of taxation and public spending should not be 'determined by economic science but instead by one's personal preferences for collective versus individual goods and by one's philosophical approach to equality.'[104]

We not only need higher taxation to fund more social goods, sharing the benefits of increased productivity between individual consumption and collective provision, but we also need an investment approach to how that spending is used. Over time if we take an investment approach to our expenditure, and focus it to deal with causes rather than symptoms we can expect to find that certain pressures on tax – for crime, stress, obesity and so on will reduce. Relatedly, if the economic system is reformed so that we have better quality growth this will reduce the damage that the economic system causes to people and the environment, which will reduce the amount of 'corrective' spending that is required. How we raise and spend revenue has a major effect on how much future revenue is needed. For example, spending on climate change now reduces the future need for expensive flood defences. Measures to make it easier to walk or cycle will reduce childhood obesity and therefore reduce future NHS costs.

At present, in the run up to the next Comprehensive Spending Review, there is something of a phoney war going on between those who believe tax levels need to be 41 per cent of GDP and those who believe they need to be at 42 per cent.[105] The Treasury's own forecasts show that to merely maintain present welfare levels, tax will need to rise to something between 45 per cent and 47 per cent of GDP by 2050.[106] This puts into perspective present debates about tax levels. But this will still allow the amount of disposable (post tax) income to rise much faster. Indeed one of the main causes behind the rising cost of maintaining present levels of welfare is that productivity will be rising elsewhere in the economy, making labour intensive welfare services, whose productivity inherently cannot rise as fast, relatively costly to maintain. But this rising productivity elsewhere in the economy also provides the solution, allowing higher taxation levels yet rising levels of disposable income. If we wish to increase the kinds and quality of public services that we want – as outlined in this and the other Programme for Renewal books – this will certainly cost more and thus require greater revenues. We should therefore aim to allow the share of taxation in GDP to rise continuously over time, towards Scandinavian levels, allowing us to fund far better quality public goods.

There are a number of issues which need to be dealt with to make the case for higher taxation. UK citizens want European style welfare and public services but on US style taxation. This is the source of the constant focus on efficiency in public services. There needs to be more honesty from government to the public that better public services will require more investment alongside management reforms. Polling also shows that whilst most people have a positive experience of public services, they tend to believe that they have had a lucky experience. They believe in general that public services and social goods are in a poor state and they also lack confidence in government's ability to do anything about it. This perception needs to be addressed head on – public services have improved in the last decade because of improved investment.

There is also a myth that the basic rate of income tax somehow represents a unique barometer for the health of the economy, so that increases in income tax under any circumstances will be disastrous. In fact there is very little relation between the basic rate of income tax and the strength of the economy according to traditional measures such as GDP. What matters is the over-all impact of the tax burden on the distribution of income (which is very different from the impact of income tax, as many indirect taxes are regressive).[107] Additionally, crude analysis of the relationship between tax (or public spending) as a share of GDP and economic growth shows very little obvious correlation.[108] It is what the revenues from tax are spent on, and how the revenue is raised, that matters for economic performance, rather than the over-all aggregate level of taxation.

There are a number of principles that should underlie the progressive approach to taxation. First, we should make the over-all tax burden progressive rather than regressive, as it is at present. Secondly, we should move towards green taxation, but in ways that do not hit the poor hardest. Thirdly, we need greater taxation on wealth and inheritance: wealth inequality is rising and has major effects on people's life chances and on the social fabric. Fourth, there needs to be more decentralisation of taxation – the only taxation under local control is Council Tax which gives only around 5 per cent of all tax receipts. This fits the devolution programme outlined in *Democracy and the Public Realm*. Finally, we should aim for tax simplification where possible, but not at the cost of our other objectives.

Taxation for redistribution

As outlined earlier, there are high levels of poverty in the UK, and inequality has risen greatly in the last twenty years. As pointed out by the Fabian Society, one in five children live in poverty, one in fifty cannot afford a winter coat, and chances in life are grotesquely unequal for children from different backgrounds.[109] *The Good Society* contains a fuller analysis of poverty and inequality, and therefore that analysis is not repeated here. It puts forward a number of policies for dealing with poverty and inequality including backing the Fabian Society's call for a Life Chances Litmus test. This volume builds on the approach of *The Good Society* by making recommendations in relation to taxation. Of course financial redistribution is not enough – people should be provided with high quality universal public services – but it is important for creating a good society.

Research shows that individuals report themselves as less happy when living in a society where inequality is high, even after controlling for their own individual income.[110] Some research suggests that the psycho-social stresses and strains produced by the experience of inequality – even for those at the upper end of the hierarchy – has a demonstrable effect on average levels of health and life expectancy.[111] Therefore we are all worse off living in an unequal society. Redistribution can create a fairer society, and it is of particular importance in an hourglass economy, where more and more workers suffer a new level of insecurity.

People strongly believe in a fair society. Research shows that when presented with a variety of tax and spend packages, 89 per cent of people prefer packages that are redistributive.[112] The tax burden measured over all – taking all direct and indirect taxes together – is regressive.[113] This is not very well known. It is roughly proportional over the middle 80 per cent of the income distribution, but the bottom 10 per cent pays more as a share of their income than average, and the top 10 per cent pays less than average. The bottom fifth of households pay 36.4 per cent of their income in taxes whilst the top fifth pay 35.6 per cent. A key objective must be to re-weight the balance of tax so that the over-all burden is progressive. What kinds of measures could help to achieve this?

The number and level of specific tax allowances should be reduced, since these primarily benefit higher earners and do not reach the poorest, in particular pension relief. Presently the top ten per cent of earners get half of the pension tax relief. We should consider moving to a single rate of tax relief at the basic rate. We should reform the local tax system to make it progressive. Council Tax is one of the most regressive parts of the current tax system. In its place we should consider a tax on land values as was explored in chapter 8.[114] We could also close the 'kink' in the current income tax/National Insurance schedules, whereby the marginal rate changes from 33 per cent to 23 per cent then to 41 per cent, by getting rid of the Upper Earnings Limit.[115] We could also increase progressive taxation through a combined top income tax/National Insurance rate of 50 per cent, on incomes of £100,000 or more per year.[116]

The specific design of reform is, however, a matter for debate, but the key is to ensure that the tax burden is progressive not regressive.

Environmental taxation

The general principles behind environmental taxation are sound from a progressive perspective. Green taxes discourage activity which is harmful to the environment and can raise revenue which can be used either to fund elements of public spending or to reduce taxation elsewhere. Public understanding of this is rising, and 63 per cent of people have said they approve of green taxes to discourage behaviour that harms the environment.[117]

We should shift to environmental taxation, but make sure that the over-all impact of the tax system is progressive. People should pay for their use of those things that are part of our environmental commons.[118] Land value taxation is an important component of this. Chapter 4 explored in detail the possibility of an energy tax and of taxes in the area of transport. A tax on domestic waste could also be used: it can be less regressive than an energy tax.[119]

It should be noted that the idea of moving taxation from 'goods' (such as work) to 'bads' is not inherently progressive, as the poorest do not pay income tax at all. We need to supplement progressive green taxation with progressive eco-spending. Green tax breaks should not be given to the well off (e.g. on solar panels), but should be designed so that they benefit the poorest (e.g. insulation grants).

Wealth and inheritance

Inequalities in wealth dwarf inequalities in income and the UK has become significantly more unequal over the last two decades. There is a clear social justice case for taxing wealth as well as income. The common complaint that this is 'double taxation' is not a good argument against this – after all, taxes on consumption such as VAT are also a form of double taxation and these are not disputed.

In general, transaction taxes – e.g. Stamp Duty on house purchases and Stamp Duty on share purchases – are not 'horizontally equitable' (someone who moves house every year pays a lot more tax than someone who stays in the same house for 10 years, for example) and are particularly distortionary as regards economic activity. Therefore we should move away from these kinds of taxes and towards taxes on holdings of wealth (inheritance tax being the exception, as this is an involuntary transfer due to death.)

We should consider a tax on all the components of individual/household wealth (as was proposed but never implemented in the 1970s in the UK) – such taxes are used successfully in other countries such as France and Switzerland, and indeed, prior to the 1997 election, the Labour Party considered proposals for an annual tax of 1-2 per cent or more on personal wealth above £100,000 (or family wealth above £200,000).[120]

We should also look at reforming inheritance tax as a way to pay for the free long term care which was proposed in *The Good Society*. At present people face a lottery: if their parent dies suddenly and leaves them a property they inherit a lot. If alternatively their parent needs long-term care it may mean all of the parent's resources are spent on this and therefore nothing is inherited. This makes it impossible to plan for our financial future. But we could pool our risk by reforming inheritance tax to pay for long-term care. We should also explore the idea that the recipients of inheritance should be taxed rather than estates,[121] and a wider capital receipts tax.[122]

A different kind of mechanism to tax wealth is a share levy, where companies would pay tax in the form of their shares. This form of taxation has the major advantage that it does not affect a company's cash flow and thus its ability to invest, as the company donates shares rather than pays cash. Companies employing more than 30 workers, or with a turnover of over £10 million, would contribute shares worth 10 per cent of their annual profits each year. This would have the effect of subtracting from the value of shares in the company by less than one per cent a year, but would allow the public to acquire a stake in economic growth that could be used for redistributive and social purposes. Such a scheme has been proposed as an example of how we could fund future pension provision.[123]

Avoidance and evasion

More attention needs to be placed on tax evasion, which costs much more than benefit fraud, although the latter is given greater attention. One way to do this might be for government to produce an annual statement of lost revenue, which estimates where money has been lost. Having tax evasion and benefit fraud figures in one place would show the relative magnitudes of the problems that we face. Britain has a series of tax loopholes which are exploited by the very wealthy. Around 60,000 of the richest people in the UK use expensive lawyers and accountants to avoid tax using these legal loopholes, costing at least £25 billion in lost revenue. There is no reason why rich footballers, pop stars and city dealers should not be meeting their tax obligations like everybody else does, and these loopholes – particularly rules around residency – should be addressed.[124]

Corporate taxation

Wealth generation is dependent upon a large economic and social infrastructure. Corporation tax is a way of enterprises paying for that infrastructure – including an educated and healthy workforce, transport systems and the rule of law – which enable them to generate wealth.

Over all, the existing corporate tax regime needs to be simplified. A lot of the tax regimes surrounding smaller firms appear to generate extra complexity without corresponding benefits to UK economic performance. (However, in some areas of corporate tax there is more justification for complexity – in particular the Research and Development tax credit has been shown to assist research and development expenditure by firms.) At the same time, however, there needs to be a strengthening of tax regulation and transparency, given the rise in mechanisms to avoid tax. For example Philip Green has used a combination of tax avoidance laws and tax havens such as Jersey to save £280 million of tax on payment of a dividend from his Arcadia group for the benefit of his wife who lives in Monaco.[125] Rupert Murdoch's News Corporation has hardly paid any tax in the UK since the late 1980s, through using a series of offshore subsidiaries. There is plenty of technical work on what dealing with tax avoidance might practically entail, including a general anti-avoidance principle and strengthened disclosure rules, but what is required is the political will to make this happen.[126]

There should be exploration of some kind of tax on excessive corporate restructuring, in order to dampen this form of activity, which increases the feeling of insecurity in the economy. There should also be an exploration of tax breaks for socially and environmentally friendly activity and tax penalties for bad behaviour. At present such tax breaks tend to follow organisational form (e.g. be awarded to charities). Instead they could follow activity. In other words good performance (e.g. in training the workforce or alleviating poverty) can be rewarded and bad behaviour (e.g. in harming the environment) can be taxed, no matter whether it is a charity or a private company engaging in those behaviours.

Following this approach, we should consider increasing corporation taxes across the board, and then reducing them when corporations meet social and environmental standards. Those who do not meet the standards would have to either absorb the higher corporation tax levels, or pass on the costs, making their products more expensive and less competitive. This system would put the onus on companies to prove that they are continuing to meet these standards, rather than placing pressure and cost on the government to maintain social and environmental policing. It would be consistent with this approach to use Statutory Training in sectors where a voluntary approach to workforce skills has not delivered results, as was proposed in *The Good Society*.

There is some evidence of a downward trend in corporate tax rates over the last 10 to 15 years across OECD economies as a whole.[127] This is fundamentally a 'beggar-my-neighbour' policy: whilst cutting corporate tax rates may increase a given economy's corporate tax revenue if other countries maintain their rates at the previous level, it is not possible for all countries to experience an increase in corporate tax revenues if they all cut their tax rates. To deal with this problem, in the long term, corporate tax policy needs to be co-ordinated at a fundamentally higher level than the nation state – first the EU level and then globally (in the same way that the Kyoto protocol attempts to address climate change in a global framework). In the short term we should improve automatic information exchange between countries by building on the European Savings Tax Directive, which would help to reduce avoidance.

A spatially balanced development

Behind the generally upward trends for growth, employment and knowledge industries lie major and widening economic disparities between and within regions. This leaves many individuals and communities without a fair chance to succeed – which is both a severe injustice to them and a major loss to the rest of society. At the same time, the over-concentration of economic growth in restricted areas of London and the South East is economically, socially and environmentally dysfunctional. A more evenly balanced spread of economic activity and development would be of benefit to all, including through easing housing pressures in the South East.[128]

Since 1997, there has been an unprecedented and welcome focus on regeneration, economic development and tackling disadvantage. However, despite some successes, there has been a failure to develop a coherent approach to tackle the underlying causes of disadvantage, poverty and inequality. Most disturbingly, the gap between affluent communities and disadvantaged communities continues to grow.

Changing this requires restoring a robust regional policy that redirects job and investment opportunities, redoubles welfare redistribution measures and couples them to real growth opportunities in the mainstream economy.[129] Above all, it means tackling the national policy choices, and growth dynamics in the prosperous regions, that constantly suck resources and wealth away from the rest of the nation. If necessary this would mean halting further expansion in the growth areas and relocating enterprise, government, and national scientific, technological and cultural investment towards the poorer regions. This kind of one-nation politics of regeneration would provide material support to individuals and communities in order to enhance their means and opportunities for social and geographical mobility. In other words it represents the spatial dimension of a longer term redistribution of resources, wealth and income.

Such an approach requires 'bottom-up' industrial policy to create employment and growth opportunities for local people in deprived areas. It could use community development funds in regions affected by manufacturing decline to support retraining and manage the social costs of economic restructuring, and maximise scope for investment incentives and other forms of regional support allowed by EU rules. We need new thinking on how to create more resilient local economies. Part of this will require a better understanding of the institutional diversity required at local and regional economic levels, including ways in which the UK can create and sustain more medium sized firms. We also need to find better ways of embedding inward investment and understanding how to keep money flowing in the local economy. All of this will require a more active local government – ideas for how to devolve more power to local government are put forward in *Democracy and the Public Realm*.

As part of this approach we could also make smarter use of procurement, to make sure that decisions are based on social and environmental criteria rather than on price – whereby the goods that are apparently the cheapest are procured, leaving externalities to be picked up by another budget.[130] The UK public sector spends £125 billion a year in procuring goods and services. If just 10 per cent of this were redirected at purchasing from the UK's poorest areas, this would be an injection of £12.5 billion into those areas, more than 17 times the annual spend on regeneration.

There also needs to be consideration of mechanisms for more democratic control, and involvement of people in decision-making at the local and regional levels. One important aspect of this is that Regional Development Agencies need better structures of accountability. There might also be experimentation with civil society groups playing a greater role in representing the needs of the local community at that level – for example as active stakeholders, both with the private sector (e.g. feeding into company decision making on local issues), and with the public sector (e.g. encouraging mechanisms such as democratic budgeting).

Changing monetary and fiscal frameworks to create more industrial democracy, fair taxation that can fund better public goods, and the reshaping of growth so that it is regionally balanced are major steps in creating a progressive political economy.

11 Social Europe

The area where we have the most power to act is at European level, where structures already exist. It is likely that by 2030 China will be the world's biggest economy, with the US the second largest and India the third. To have a place at the negotiation table we will need to be represented as Europe not as Britain. No European country is big enough to shape markets alone, but together Europe can work to achieve the creation of a democratic economy that promotes well-being, social justice and environmental sustainability.

Europe must be more than a purely economic union. The recent focus on market liberalisation needs to be rebalanced with action to build a social Europe which regulates and shapes markets in the public interest. The Lisbon Agenda has social, environmental and economic objectives, but at present the focus has been primarily on growth and competitiveness. There is a need for a rebalancing of the strategy towards the social and environmental.

Whilst there is no such thing as a single 'European social model', there are common values and a commitment to publicly funded services, redistributive systems of taxation, universal entitlements and regulation of workplaces to protect worker rights and promote industrial democracy. The neo-liberal perspective argues that this kind of social market creates inefficiency and has led to low growth and high unemployment in some European economies. This view is wrong: there is no evidence of any relationship between traditional economic performance measures and levels of taxation or labour market regulation. Indeed the Swedish and Finnish economies are in the top three of the latest World Economic Forum competitiveness tables and are some of the most regulated and highly taxed economies in the world, whilst the United States is sixth.[131] They also top the world's quality of life tables whereas the US is in fifteenth place.[132]

The UK needs to be more humble in lecturing to Europe. Our politicians often call for European countries to learn the lessons from our economy. But we should also be learning lessons from European social models. To take just one example, output per hour worked is nearly 30 per cent higher in France and more than 10 per cent higher in Germany than in the UK.[133] Productivity is not an end in itself, but these productivity differences throw into relief our 'low road' economy based on low investment and low skills in contrast with 'higher road' economies.

The UK in Europe

The challenge of shaping the global economy cannot be met through acting purely at the national level. Whilst national governments do retain some power, major changes can only come through nation states acting together in concert, as markets continue to put pressure on progressive policies for redistribution and public investment. The need to keep financial markets happy affects all of a government's policies, not just its monetary and fiscal policies. It affects its employment policies, its industrial policies, its social policies, its environmental policies, its education policies – because all these are factored into financial markets' assessment of the 'political risk' attached to investments in a particular economy.[134] The ability of private investors to disinvest and reinvest somewhere else in response to such risk assessments allows them to drive a harder bargain with the labour movements and wider electorates of those economies. Research has concluded that 'Over the long run, international financial integration tends to favor capital over labor, especially in developed countries'.[135]

For the UK this means that greater European integration is important for creating a good economy. There are some strong arguments in favour of joining the euro at an appropriate time when our economy is sufficiently synchronised with the rest of Europe.[136] It would enable us to be part of an economic force that is strong enough to act on the world stage. The euro would provide gains in trade at the European level through the removal of the exchange rate risk with our largest export markets. It would also enable the UK to move out of its low skills-low investment equilibrium, as the greater stability provided by the removal of exchange rate risk would enable employers to engage in investment with more certainty, as is the case in France and Germany.[137] This would also help preserve our manufacturing sector, which has lost half of its employment levels since 1997.

The main concern that opponents of monetary union have is that of losing exchange rate flexibility and having a single interest rate which applies to such a large area. They argue that exchange rates should move to trade into balance – if a country imports more than it exports, its currency should drop in value, making exports cheaper and bringing trade back to balance through stabilising export prices. The evidence suggests, however, that the sterling exchange rate does not change in ways that is helpful to our trade position. The relative price of UK goods has fluctuated wildly over the last 30 years. This is because exchange rates are now determined far more by speculative financial flows, which are in excess of £300 trillion, than by trade, which is valued at less than £10 trillion. Concerns about interest rate policy are crucial. Even the Bank of England has to set interest rates that trade off interests of different regions (booming South East, depressed North East). The solution to this may be better regional policy, but at the EU level there will be even bigger differences that uniform monetary policy may find it difficult to deal with.

Given the importance and the complexity of the issue, there needs to be a proper and public debate about joining the euro rather than the curious silence over the past few years. It is important that the debate does not descend into nationalistic symbolism but is a serious discussion about the economic, social and political implications of euro membership.

European economic policy

Economic policies at the EU level need to be rebalanced. They have increasingly focused upon a neo-liberal economic agenda, based on liberalisation, flexible labour markets and more competition. These policies are not sufficient to stabilise economic activity nor deal with unemployment – they have not dealt with the recession that many countries have been in since 2001. Some European politicians and the European Central Bank have argued that this is because of a lack of flexibility in labour, product and capital markets and point to the UK and US. But this analysis misses out the stimuli that have been applied in the UK and US through public spending. Since 2000 public spending in the UK has increased significantly, which has been crucial in sustaining UK growth and employment. Levels of unemployment in many member states are dangerously high, averaging 8 per cent in the EU as a whole, and 9 per cent in the eurozone, with 17 per cent of those under 25 being out of work. The European Central Bank is sometimes accused to being obsessed with inflation to the detriment of taking a more expansionary approach to help deal with unemployment. In fact it has behaved as if it has a symmetrical interest rate policy (trying to keep inflation neither too high nor too low) and has even cut rates when inflation has been above 2 per cent. Similarly sometimes the Stability and Growth Pact is accused of preventing countries from spending when they need to reflate their economy through the 3 per cent deficit limit. Again, in practice, the member states take a pragmatic approach as shown by Germany and France having repeatedly breached the ceiling without sanction, but the UK government remains of the view that 'the Stability and Growth Pact does not appear to have supported counter-cyclical policy in recent years'.[138] There is room for further reform of the pact in order to reduce pressure on member states to reign in public spending, but it is not easy for the UK to influence that debate from the outside.

Domestic demand needs to be stimulated in the Eurozone countries. This could be done at the European level as well as the member state level, for example through issuing Eurobonds and the creation of a European Recovery Fund as advocated by Gordon Brown in the 1990s. In the present circumstances positive action in the form of increased public expenditure could raise demand to a higher level and enable national economies to run at a lower level of unemployment. Such measures need to be carefully judged to create confidence in continued expansion and thus encourage firms to increase their capacity and employ more workers. Coordination is also needed among member countries to take account of the fact that as countries' economies become more closely integrated, changes in demand in one country have an increasing effect on their trading neighbours. European capacity for expansion is important not only to reduce unemployment but also to counteract the danger of world recession posed by the US external deficit.

Refocusing the union

There needs to be a refocus on social and environmental objectives, which are presently subordinated to economic policy and are not always consistent with it.[139] This is a major policy agenda beyond the scope of this paper but requires the kinds of policies put forward in the Programme for Renewal at the European level, including redistribution, better regulated markets and environmental taxation and regulation. There should be a greater focus on poverty reduction through the creation of a European anti-poverty programme. Following the Open Method of Co-ordination all member states should prepare anti-poverty strategies, but the strategies of lower income countries could be part financed through EU funding. Further, the EU could put forward minimum standards in the main areas of public services such as housing and health, and in other welfare areas such as working time, whilst leaving it to member states to choose suitable policy instruments to institutionalise them. A refocus on collective schemes as a solution to pensions is also required, rather than reliance on purely market-based approaches. European environmental policy needs to move much further in adopting legally binding targets for greenhouse gas emissions. It should regulate more strongly in relation to environmental hazards, and seek to promote more sustainable production and consumption. There should be promotion of decentralised energy sources, low energy buildings and better public transport infrastructures, mirroring the approach laid out in this volume at the European level. To take all of these measures forward, the European budget would also need to increase over time.

Managing globalisation through the EU

There are many ways in which the EU could help manage globalisation for the benefit of its members and the wider world.[140] Europe needs to use its leverage to push for the kind of global economic system outlined in the next chapter. For example a system of managed exchange rates and capital controls could help to reduce the negative impacts of speculative financial flows and the instability which could come if the dollar were to collapse. Similarly, Europe could push for a new system to manage global trade imbalances, a new global reserves system and new approaches to intellectual property as described in the next chapter. Europe has the power to do this as the euro is beginning to compete with the dollar as a global reserve currency.

The EU should significantly strengthen its role in supporting poorer economies and reducing poverty. As well as increasing the quantity and quality of aid, it should look at developing new funding streams to achieve the UN's Millennium Development Goals. A foreign exchange transaction tax or a levy on international air travel could be used. Even greater in impact would be using 'contraction and convergence' as described in the next chapter. This would 'pre-distribute' tradeable carbon quotas on a global scale and would be highly beneficial to poor people who have very low emissions.

The EU needs to supplement existing development programmes with more work on strengthening democracy in poorer countries – enabling them to build a free press, parliaments, and active civil societies, so that they can engage in their own process of development. If we wish to help poorer countries, we also need to get our own house in order on matters which have negative impacts on poorer countries such as climate change, tax havens, money laundering and aid conditionality.

A large part of aid given by European countries to poorer countries is 'phantom aid'.[141] Phantom aid includes money which is tied to purchases from the donor country's own firms, the double-counting of debt relief, and aid which has excessive administrative and reporting costs. Europe should work to improve the quality of aid given to poor countries through an International Aid Agreement which contains minimum standards, including untying aid.

Another area for exploration is that of creating minimum global social and environmental standards which can be integrated into the World Trade Organisation rules (subject to the WTO being reformed as described in the next chapter). This could help to stem any 'race to the bottom' of standards where employers in poor countries unfairly exploit their workers and the environment. Freer trade should be seen as a means, not an end in itself. It should be supported only in so far as it advances social goals. For example, under current WTO rules countries are in general not allowed to set restrictions on how imported goods are made, since this would restrict competition. One result of this is that if the UK sets farmers higher animal welfare standards which add to their costs, more meat is imported from countries that do not have to meet our welfare standards. The net result could well be more animal cruelty – as well as more food transport and poorer British farmers. This is the result if one takes the view that the only goal of trade is to let people buy products at the lowest possible price.

The way products are produced is, however, a legitimate concern of governments, and they should be allowed to set the same public-good standards on imports that they set for domestic production – including employment conditions, environmental standards, and a range of appropriate standards in other areas, such as safety and animal welfare. In order to avoid the charge of protectionism these minimum standards should be set at realistic levels, and then could be raised over time as poor countries grew richer.

At the same time the EU should also work to open its markets further to poorer countries, and to reduce its unfair agricultural subsidies which distort the market, particularly the Common Agricultural Policy and the sugar regime. Many CAP payments across European countries go to large multinational companies and the largest farmers, rather than in protecting small farmers.[142]

Finally, the UK should seek better exchange with other policy-makers in Europe. The UK has tended to look over the Atlantic for policy inspiration. We have lots we could share with European partners, such as our experience in pensions reform, competition policy, reform of agricultural subsidies and the climate change levy. But we also have lots to learn from our partners in Europe, including on issues such as public transport, skills and education, health, industrial policy and the social model. By sharing the best from different countries' thinking we can build a social Europe that can help shape a better global political economy.

12 Progressive globalisation

We cannot consider the national economy in isolation – we are part of a global economy. Therefore creating a democratic economy focused on well-being, social justice and environmental sustainability needs change to happen at the international level. The major challenge we face is to manage globalised and financialised capitalism for the good of the many not the few. Many of the ideas in this section are of a visionary and longer term nature, but moving towards them is fundamental to creating the economy that we want.

As capitalism becomes global, so must the forces to democratise it. The aim must be to regulate capitalism in such a way that it can provide a high quality of life for all. Economic globalisation has outpaced political globalisation. Unregulated capitalism is chasing regulation out of its few remaining hiding places. The tables need to be turned: there are only a finite number of places that unregulated capitalism can go to, and we need to chase it until it runs out of places to hide. To do this we need to move towards an ambitious programme of global governance and change, through new international institutions and frameworks and stronger civil society at the global level, including more linkages between trade unions internationally and greater links with progressive social movements, especially in poor countries.

The truth about globalisation

Globalisation is a complex phenomenon which is creating multiple changes, but it is not beyond the control of governments. Both the right and the left have argued that government has few options in the face of globalisation, but this has been too easy a way to escape responsibility. On the contrary, globalisation is a political phenomenon which is shaped by political action and power.

It has differential impacts on different groups. The international mobile elite class have gained from globalisation in terms of better opportunities, travel and higher salaries. But for most people globalisation has not been so positive. A set of people are excluded from markets entirely, and globalisation has not helped them. The working and middle classes have been most affected by the insecurities and uncertainties which have come about through globalisation and market liberalisation. In particular, the global labour force has doubled in size through the entry of China, India and the former Soviet Union to market capitalism. This has put a downward pressure on wages in relation to capital. Hence low-skilled workers have been hit hard by globalisation. The argument put forward by neo-liberals is that UK people will benefit from low prices and from demand from Asia. The problem with this classic free trade theory is timing – in the long run this might or might not be true, but the process of adjustment could take decades and this will be very destabilising in the form of unemployment and withdrawal of the welfare state.[143]

Contrary to the neo-liberal position, globalisation has not been very good at generating growth, or poverty and inequality reduction.[144] During the era of managed capitalism from 1960 to 1978 the world growth rate was 2.7 per cent. From 1979 to 2000 the world growth rate almost halved to 1.5 per cent. Income inequality between countries has fallen since 1980, but this result is due solely to rising incomes in China, and China's approach to capitalism has not been based on anything like a neo-liberal model. Latin America shows the real failure of neo-liberal economic policies. During the 1990s many Latin American countries took on neo-liberal economics under the guidance of the IMF and World Bank. But initial growth was based upon borrowing and the sale of national assets, and thereafter growth petered out and was replaced by recession. We have seen the rise of leftist governments in the region as a response to the failure of neo-liberal economics. In Argentina there was growth of over 8 per cent per annum for three years after the country became free of the IMF programme.

Absolute income gaps are growing widely: the absolute incomes of the top 20 per cent of the world are shooting away from everybody else. Research shows that for every £100 of growth between 1981 and 2001, only £1.30 went to reduce dollar a day poverty;[145] and over half of world growth during the 1990s accrued to the richest 10 per cent of the population. Therefore the present form of globalisation does not seem to lead to decreases in inequality or poverty.

Globalisation as promoted at the moment is increasing the power of finance capital and multinational companies in relation to many national governments and civil society. There is a need to swing the pendulum back. We need a politics of 'global social democracy'.[146] How do we democratise the global economy and make it fair and sustainable? There are many ideas we can take forward.[147]

Trade and investment

First, we could review the role of the IMF and World Bank, created more than fifty years ago, and now operating in a very different economic context. Part of any reform should enable poorer countries more power to set their own economic policies.[148] Successful economies have tended not to follow neo-liberal prescriptions: India is highly interventionist, China has maintained capital controls and other state direction. America runs external deficits by way of the dollar's international reserve status that no other country could.[149] This is not to say that liberalisation is always a bad thing, but that what works will be different in different countries.

The World Trade Organisation (WTO) also needs to become more transparent and provide more support to poorer countries. Poor countries tend to have very limited resources to engage in trade negotiations. We should expand the WTO legal advisory centre, to strengthen the capacity of poorer countries to engage in WTO processes, including bringing and defending WTO disputes. National parliaments should have greater power to scrutinise WTO policy-making, WTO documentation should be made more transparent and available on the web, and there should be greater rights for civil society organisations to make representations to the organisation.

Research shows that the benefits of Foreign Direct Investment (FDI) – which was seen as a miracle economic drug during the 1990s – are exaggerated.[150] The effects of FDI can be positive, neutral or negative, and they are generally negative for the poorest countries. Positive effects happen when accompanied by interventionist government policies. There needs to be more focus on an economy's 'internal integration' rather than on its external integration with other economies.[151] This implies an economy with dense links between sectors and with strong domestic demand, which creates a positive spiral between production, consumption and wages.

Trade is a crucial part of the global economy, but trade favours the strong and the rules are written by and stacked in the favour of richer countries and corporate lobbies. Trade rules mean that poor countries have had to open their markets to rich countries, but not the other way around. There has been a focus on capital liberalisation rather than increasing cross-border labour mobility, which would have been of greater benefit to poor countries. We should move towards asymmetric trade policies which allow poorer countries to access rich markets but give them time limited protections over their own markets. Rich and middle-income countries should open up their markets fully to poor countries. Poor countries should have the right to use tariffs to develop their own nascent economies – growing their industrial sector is a major source of innovation and revenue. Eighty-five per cent of people in Britain believe that Britain should 'argue vigorously' within the EU for reforms of EU trading practices to make them fairer for poorer countries – even when reminded that current practices benefit British industry and jobs.[152] This should be complemented with encouraging more regional trade: some middle-income countries are the biggest offenders for anti-poor protectionism. Trade unions in rich countries should work with unions in poorer countries to develop policy demands which all can agree upon as fair, rather than working against one another.

International trade could also be used proactively as a tool of climate responsibility. Imports from countries which refuse to participate in international agreements to tackle climate change could be charged a climate tariff to buy carbon offsets for their production. This could be waived for exporting companies which themselves pursue effective, independently audited climate programmes. There is precedent for using trade measures to protect the environment, established by a case that the United States brought against Thailand at the WTO. Such measures could have powerful effects on the US, which has thus far had no incentive to cut emissions under the Kyoto Protocol.[153]

All countries also need to be careful of the extension of trade agreements. In particular GATS (the General Agreement on Trade in Services) took effect in 1995 and requires members to further liberalise trade in services. GATS came about primarily due to the lobbying of multinational companies. There is increasing focus on targeting public services such as health, education and utilities to make them tradeable for profit. This makes it much more difficult for local and national communities to regulate public services to meet policy goals. These agreements are not necessarily in the interests of any society – it is corporations that stand to benefit. Negotiations are conducted remotely and secretively at the WTO – the EU tabled its offer of service liberalisation under GATS in June 2005 without publicity. Once they take force, these liberalisations are permanent and enforceable by economic sanctions by the World Trade Organisation. We should instead focus upon creating a General Agreement on Public Services (GAPS).[154] This would set binding standards that could be converted into law by duly constituted institutions at international, national and sub-national levels. It would also promote good practice by providing benchmarks with which civil society campaigns could hold accountable international institutions, governments and service providers.

Trade reform should be combined with debt relief. There is now greater awareness of the problem of crushing debt, where poor countries face high levels of repayment which prevent them from spending money on basic public welfare such as health and education, which in turn prohibits development. The case for debt cancellation is strong, and rich countries should go much further in cancelling debt. We should also introduce international insolvency laws to help countries which cannot meet their repayments to restructure their debts.[155]

The role played by multinational companies in the global economy is a complex one, but it is clear that governance structures need to catch up with the international nature of the companies. There is a lot of work on codes of conduct for corporations which should continue, and they need to become better implemented and more enforceable.[156] Such codes of conduct need to extend both to Western countries and to the increasingly powerful corporations based in emerging economies such as China and India. One area where there is a particular need for action is to make corporate lobbying more transparent. The EU, US and WTO amongst others are all guilty of giving corporate lobbyists privileged access.[157] They should introduce more transparency in how they are lobbied, and corporations should disclose their lobbying positions and funding of think tanks, trade associations and other campaigns to influence policy.

Intellectual property

Intellectual property, such as copyright or patents, creates monopoly rights for the owner. The purpose of intellectual property law should be to promote innovation and the sharing of knowledge. Knowledge is a public good and should be made available unless there are good arguments to restrict it. Shakespeare, Aristotle and Leonardo da Vinci were motivated to create their great work without the alleged incentive of intellectual property. Intellectual property has always had dangers and its scope has grown greatly, to the point where it now reins back innovation. For example the aeroplane was not being developed beyond prototype in the early part of the twentieth century, as patents which were owned by the Wright brothers and others. This deadlock was only broken by government intervention when World War 1 required the development of the plane. Today we have seen the realm of patents extend to computer software, the gene and on yoga positions.

The benefit that accrues has been to corporations, not to knowledge and innovation. It was US corporations which pushed for TRIPS (Trade-Related Aspects of Intellectual Property Rights) in 1994. These overrode national intellectual property law and led to the creation of enforceable intellectual property law internationally. The rights that were put forward were not in the best interests of societies in rich or poor countries, but of corporate power – particularly the pharmaceuticals industry. We have seen this particularly in relation to generic life-saving drugs in poor countries. The current regime leads to little research being done around the creation of affordable life-saving drugs, as these are not lucrative enough. And charges for existing drugs tend to be ridiculously high. Those medicines which are essential should be provided to poor countries at cost – there is no additional cost for rich countries in doing this. More widely, we should set up an innovation fund – a prize fund that rewards researchers for discoveries to deal with problems that poorer countries face.[158] The size of the prize would be related to the importance of the discovery. All discoveries could then be kept in the public domain, leading to maximum innovation. We should also create an agreement to protect traditional knowledge and resources in poor countries, such as local medicinal knowledge, from being stolen through patents. Examples of this abound – for example the American attempts to patent turmeric or basmati rice in the 1990s.

Technological change and the rise of 'open source' developments such as software (e.g. Linux) and knowledge banks (e.g. Wikipedia) also force us to rethink the intellectual property laws of the nineteenth and twentieth century, and to develop those which can deal with more creative commons. As a response to this and the wider issues discussed, governments should adopt the RSA's Adelphi Charter on creativity, innovation and intellectual property.[159] This puts forward a set of principles on intellectual property which focus upon the public interest.

Re-embedding capital

Capital liberalisation has not lived up to its theoretical promise.[160] Rather than allocate capital from rich economies to poor ones, in fact it has moved in the opposite direction. It has increased systemic risk in the financial system through devices such as derivatives, even though they were designed to reduce risk. And capital liberalisation has not led to faster growth and more investment.

'Capital controls' is a generic term used to cover a range of policy instruments that have the effect of limiting, slowing or discouraging the movement of capital across national borders. During the post-war 'Golden Age' every economy in the world (bar the US and Switzerland) operated extensive capital controls. This was seen as an essential pillar of the international 'Bretton Woods' system designed by Keynes and others – it made possible the growth of free trade against a background of stable exchange rates and full employment. But capital controls are regarded today as something of a taboo.

There are a number of rationales for capital controls. Capital controls may limit the damage to 'real economies' caused by 'irrational' or unnecessary financial volatility. 'Hot money' has been very damaging for poor countries, for example in Asia and Latin America, when investors have withdrawn money in a panic. In the 'Asian crisis', Malaysia was the country which came out most unscathed in the region, and this was due to its use of capital controls. Capital controls may limit 'capital flight', which can undermine currencies and government bonds when full employment macropolicies are attempted. They may also limit the 'exit' options of private capital and thus increase the bargaining power of employees and others over the industrial and social contract.

Capital controls would reduce the volume of speculative currency transactions and the climate of volatility and instability they create. Such instability is clearly a problem not only for small or 'developing' economies but also for the entire global economy, which is, of course, increasingly interlinked (and not just by financial markets!). Thus the 'Asian contagion' of 1998-9 had negative reverberations that went way beyond East Asia (through Latin America and Russia to the European systems that were linked to them, for example); and any future crisis around the dollar, which many now fear, could clearly have devastating effects throughout the world economy, which would be exacerbated by speculative movements.

Capital controls are also important for restoring the ability to have expansionary Keynesian economic policy. The pressure of international financial markets imposes a 'deflationary' bias on economic policies that mitigates against full employment. Capital controls are a necessary adjunct to the expansion of free trade, because they allow the dislocations of employment that free trade produces to be cushioned by full employment policies. As argued earlier, all of a government's policies are affected by the need to keep the organisations trading in financial markets happy. Left-Labour governments almost always attract a 'risk premium' in financial markets, which is typically reflected in the higher interest rates they need to maintain to keep other things equal.[161]

There are a number of practical ways in which capital controls could be used by countries. They could simply use temporary capital controls, or could use a foreign exchange transactions tax. This could be set at two levels – a lower level to raise revenues, which could be moved to a higher level if there were a crisis, to raise the cost of debilitating money flows. At the lower level it could be used to raise funds for global public goods, and at the higher level to regulate international financial flow. Whilst in the past it has been assumed that this would need to be adopted internationally, this is no longer the case, as all trades in any one currency are settled through its own central bank electronic clearing mechanism, which could be the place where the tax was levied.[162] By way of example, a sterling stamp duty at 0.005 per cent would raise around £1.7bn in the UK and would be difficult to avoid.

Global reserves

Trickle-down economics does not work: in the global economy money flows from poor countries to rich ones. The United States benefits from the dollar being the world's reserve currency and it borrows $2 billion a day to cover its current account deficit. Much of this is held by poor nations as part of their reserves. But this situation causes a number of problems.[163] While reserves help countries manage risks (e.g. to bolster confidence in their currency), the amount that countries are holding in reserve has been increasing massively, from around 8 per cent of GDP in the 1970s to nearly 30 per cent in 2004. This has a huge impact on poor countries. Reserves earn only 1-2 per cent real interest, whilst if they were used more productively they could generate real wealth or be used to fund public goods. The economic loss is immense – enough to meet the Millennium Development Goals. This also has a net effect on the global economy, reducing over-all demand, which in turn places greater demand on the US to spend more than it has to keep the global economy going – a vicious circle, leading to the precarious financial system we are in now. As the American deficit gets larger and larger, investors will increasingly lose faith in the dollar's position as a reserve currency and they will begin to shift into other currencies such as the euro or the Chinese yuan. This will put downward pressure on the dollar, which will then lead more investors to exit. As the dollar price drops, people will also pull out their money from US equities, causing a stock market fall. All of this may happen in a smooth fashion or it may happen in an instant. But the risk to the global economy from a crash is huge.

We need a new global reserves system that can create more stability and release more funding for social goods. As argued by the Fabian Society, we can revive Keynes's proposal for an international clearing union whereby trade surpluses would have to be used in a way to sustain global economic demand, allowing those with trade deficits to return their accounts to balance.[164] This would be done through creating a new global reserve system, and using a new reserve currency, which Keynes called 'bancors'. Such a system would make the international system far less unstable and would also prevent any country building up too large a trade deficit or trade surplus, as well as freeing up money for global public goods.

The political economy of the global environment

We must also deal with the central question of how we manage the environment. As part of this we will almost certainly need to engage in a programme of 'contraction and convergence' to make sure that we live within our environmental means.[165] Such a programme would set a maximum limit to carbon emissions globally (which would be reduced over time). These would be divided out between countries. Over time allocations would converge so that it was based on equal emissions for each person. The allowances would be tradeable, allowing countries with lower emissions to sell their permits to countries unable to manage with their shares. Not only would this have environmental benefits, it would also be highly redistributive as many poorer countries live well within their ecological means. It could provide a mechanism to deal with the rich countries' 'ecological debt' to poor countries – our indebtedness for the use of more than our fair share of environmental resources.

In particular, giving everybody an equal level of emissions would mean we were engaging in 'pre-distribution' rather than redistribution, as everyone in society would be given the right to something of value. This would function as a limited basic income for all, hence marrying sustainability with social justice.[166] It would also, rather neatly, be possible to make the tradeable emission allowance the currency that is used by the international clearing union proposed above.[167] Contraction and convergence seems a long way off the agenda at present, but such a programme seems like the only long-term way to secure an acceptable level of emissions at the global level.

As outlined in chapter 2, we also face the challenge of mitigating the peaking of world oil which will create a shortage of liquid fuels. Analysis shows that if a crash mitigation programme investing in alternative liquid fuels and measures to reduce demand were engaged in 20 years before oil peaking, it could prevent a liquid fuels shortage. If it is done a decade before peaking this would leave a decade of fuel shortages.[168] Worldwide oil consumption is enormous, and therefore if mitigation is too late the balance of supply and demand will be achieved through extreme shortages, which would cause serious hardship. We do not know how close we are to the oil peak, and therefore it is not easy for policy-makers to manage this risk. Nevertheless it would be sensible to begin a large-scale mitigation programme involving business, government and civil society to alleviate major problems in the future. Contraction and convergence would also help for a global managed retreat from oil dependency.

If we do not create the global structures and institutions to manage today's challenges everybody will be worse off – even the well off cannot opt out of a world threatened by climate change or financial shocks. The interconnected nature of the global economy means that any shocks will reverberate through the whole system. We need to put some fuses in the system to strengthen the global financial architecture; otherwise, when things go wrong the whole system could collapse, as it did in 1929 after the Wall Street Crash, which would be catastrophic for the prosperity of all.

The Jubilee 2000 (Drop the Debt) and Make Poverty History campaigns illustrate the power of what can be achieved when progressive forces work together. We need to campaign, and build alliances across movements: bridging political parties with civil society movements, creating links between richer and poorer countries. We must bring these agendas to the level of national governments, to make them negotiate a better globalisation on our behalf.

Afterword

Despite increased material affluence, we are living in a social recession. Markets are increasingly the master of mankind, rather than the other way around. In the good society the economy is a means to social justice, quality of life and environmental sustainability, rather than an end in itself. This volume shows what it will take to achieve a good economy.

Globally we need a different kind of globalisation which redresses imbalances of power and wealth and gives countries back their right to choose their path of development. We need to put in place mechanisms to stabilise the global financial system, make trade fair and use radical measures to protect the global environment.

At the European level we must become part of a modern social Europe which has the power to shape a fairer global economy. Europe must move away from neo-liberal policies towards a more expansionist economic approach. And Europe must not just be an economic instrument, but work to strengthen the social and environmental agenda, both at home and abroad.

Nationally we need to create an economy based on real quality of life. We must strengthen the market by regulating it properly. We should fund high quality public goods through higher levels of taxation, and redistribute to achieve a more equal society. We need to reform our housing system so that everyone has access to an affordable home and change our energy and transport systems so that we move towards sustainability.

Regionally we need a rebalancing of growth away from the South East and towards other areas. This will help ease the overheated housing market and local environmental pressures in the South East, and result in a fairer distribution of economic and social opportunities throughout the population.

Companies need to become more accountable organisations, which consider the needs of all stakeholders, and in particular focus upon the quality of work and skills of their employees. We are producers as well as consumers, and carers as well as workers. Companies should become more flexible to allow people to meet their needs to care for others.

As individuals in the good economy we will have a higher quality of life, which comes not from overwork and ever higher levels of consumption but from greater leisure time, higher quality work, and living in a healthier, happier society.

Notes

1. S. Hall, 'New Labour's Double Shuffle', *Soundings* Issue 24, Autumn 2003.

2. T. Blair, 'Europe moving forward again', *Progressive Politics* Vol 4.3, 2005.

3. R. McKibbin, in *New Left Review,* July-Aug 2000, p72.

4. Margaret Thatcher, in an interview to *The Sunday Times,* 3 May 1981.

5. Gordon Brown MP at the Oxfam Gilbert Murray Memorial Lecture, 2000.

6. P. Thompson, 'Disconnected Capitalism: Or Why Employers Can't Keep Their Side of the Bargain', *Work, Employment and Society* 17.2, 2003, 359-378.

7. B. Burchell et al, *Job Insecurity and Work Intensification*, Joseph Rowntree Foundation 1999.

8. A. Pettifor, *The Coming First World Debt Crisis*, Palgrave Macmillan 2006.

9. M. Goos and A. Manning, 'McJobs and MacJobs: The Growing Polarisation of Jobs in the UK', in R. Dickens, P. Gregg and J. Wadsworth (eds), *The Labour Market Under New Labour: The State of Working Britain*, Palgrave 2003; F. Nolan, 'The changing world of work', *Journal of Health Services Research and Policy,* 9, 1, 2004, supplement 1.

10. R. Taylor, *The Significance of the Working in Britain in 2000 survey*, ESRC 2002; D. Coats, *An Agenda for Work*, The Work Foundation 2005.

11. R. Wilkinson, *The Impact of Inequality*, Routledge 2005; World Bank, *World Development Report 2006: Equity and Development*, World Bank 2006; M. Marmot, Status Syndrome, Bloomsbury 2004.

12. S. Lansley, *Rich Britain*, Politicos 2006.

13. R. Layard, *Happiness*, Penguin 2005; H. Shah, and N. Marks, *A Well-being Manifesto for a Flourishing Society*, new economics foundation 2004.

14. M. Bunting, *Willing Slaves: How the Overwork Culture is Ruling Our Lives*, HarperCollins 2004; S. White, 'Markets, time and citizenship', *Renewal* 12:3, 2004.

15. Which, *Which? Choice: pensions*, 2005 (available online at: www.which.co.uk/files/application/pdf/0506choicepensions_rep-445-55629.pdf).

16. WWF, *Living Planet Report 2004*, WWF 2004.

17. R. Hirsch, *The Inevitable Peaking of World Oil Production*, Atlantic Council Bulletin Vol. XVI No 3, 2005.

18. C. Crouch, 'Models of capitalism', *New Political Economy*, 10, 4, 2005, 439-56.

19. A. Turner, *Just Capital: The Liberal Economy*, Macmillan 2001.

20. N. Pearce et al (eds), *Social Justice: Building a Fairer Britain*, ippr 2005.

21. S. Sachdev, *Paying the Cost: Public Private Partnerships and the public service workforce*, Catalyst 2004; P. Maltby and T. Gosling, *Ending the 'two-tier' workforce*, ippr 2003.

22. T. Burchardt, 'Just Happiness? Subjective Wellbeing and Social Policy', in N. Pearce et al (eds), *Social Justice: Building a Fairer Britain*, ippr 2005, pp252-3.

23. R. Layard, *Happiness*, Penguin 2005; H. Shah and N. Marks, *A Well-being Manifesto for a Flourishing Society*, new economics foundation 2004.

24. *Working Hours in the UK*, Chartered Institute for Personal Development 2006.

25. *Working Time Developments 2004*, European Industrial Relations Observatory 2005.

26. T. Jackson, *Chasing Progress: Beyond measuring economic growth*, Surrey University/new economics foundation 2004.

27. See www.statistics.gov.uk/hhsa/hhsa/Index.html.

28. D. Aeron Thomas et al, *Valuing what matters*, new economics foundation 2004.

29. A. Gore, 'Market Meltdown' in *Postings*, Autumn 2006, Skoll Centre/Said Business School.

30. For example see S. Himmelweit, 'Accounting for Caring', *Radical Statistics*, Winter 1998; D. Purdy, 'Markets and the Mixed Economy', *Soundings* 28, 2004.

31. N. Stern, *Stern Review on the Economics of Climate Change*, HM Treasury 2006.

32. *SERA's vision for a Progressive Energy Policy*, SERA 2006.

33. See IPPR's research – www.ippr.org.uk/pressreleases/?id=2058.

34. R. Willis, *Microgeneration*, Compass Thinkpiece 2006.

35. M. McDonald, *System Integration of Additional Micro-Generation*, SIAM 2004, commissioned by DTI/OFGEM Distributed Generation Programme.

36. Sustainable Development Commission, *The Role of Nuclear Power in a Low Carbon Economy*, Sustainable Development Commission 2006.

37. S. Cairns and C. Newson, *Predict and Decide. Aviation, climate change and UK policy*, Environmental Change Institute 2006.

38. For a historical review see N. Thompson, *Left in the Wilderness: The Political Economy of British Democratic Socialism since 1979*, Acumen 2002.

39. The Work Foundation has recently offered a working definition of the knowledge economy as 'that share of national income and employment produced by innovating organisations combining ICT and highly skilled labour to exploit global scientific, technological, and creative knowledge networks'. Of course much then hangs on how we give precise definition to these terms and attempt to measure their real instantiation. For a critical deconstruction of the diverse phenomena that have variously been brought under these headings see Ursula Huws, 'Material World: The Myth of the "Weightless Economy"', *Socialist Register* 1999.

40. Local Futures, *State of the Nation*, Local Futures Group 2006; P. Thompson, *The Knowledge Economy Myth*, 2004.

41. D. Henwood, *After the New Economy*, 2005, drawing upon Chris Benner.

42. M. O' Sullivan, *Contests for Corporate Control – Corporate Governance and Economic Performance in the United States and Germany*, Oxford University Press 2000.

43. P. Thompson, 'Disconnected capitalism: Or why employers can't keep their side of the bargain', *Work, Employment and Society* 2003.

44. OECD, *Innovation Policy and Performance: a cross-country comparison*, OECD 2005, p15.

45. C. Lloyd and J. Payne, 'On the "Political Economy of Skill": Assessing the Possibilities for a Viable High Skills Project in the United Kingdom', *New Political Economy*, 7, 3, 2002, 367-395.

46. D. Ashton and F. Green, *Education, Training and the Global Economy*, Edward Elgar 1996.

47. W. Hutton, *The World We're In*, Abacus 2002, pp138-9.

48. Office of National Statistics.

49. See R. Jeary et al, *The Future of Manufacturing*, Amicus 2006. As the report notes, however, this decline is swollen by the outsourcing of service functions within industry such as accounting and delivery services. When these activities were part of manufacturing business they were defined as manufacturing activities. Once outsourced to service companies they were recorded as part of the service sector. This may have exaggerated the fall in manufacturing by as much as 20 per cent.

50. Vivid Economics, *The Business Opportunities for SMEs in tackling the causes of Climate Change,* Shell Springboard 2006.

51. See, inter alia, L. Soley, *Leasing the Ivory Tower – The Corporate Takeover of Academia*, South End Press 1995; Slaughter & Leslie, *Academic Capitalism: Politics, Policies and the Entrepreneurial University*, John Hopkins University Press 1997; D. Bok, *Universities in the Marketplace: The commercialisation of Higher Education,* Princeton University Press 2003; Slaughter & Rhoades, *Academic Capitalism & the New Economy: Markets, States, and Higher Education,* John Hopkins University Press 2004.

52. Drahos & Braithwaite, *Information Feudalism – Who Owns the Knowledge Economy?*, WW Norton & Company 2003; C. May, 'Unacceptable Costs: The Consequences of Making Knowledge Property in a Global Society', *Global Society* Vol. 16, No.2, April 2002, pp 123-144.

53. M. Francesconi and A. Gosling, *Career paths of Part-time Workers*, Equal Opportunities Commission Working Paper No.19, 2005.

54. M. Evandrou & K. Glaser, 'Combining work and family life: the pension penalty of caring', *Ageing & Society* 23, 2003, 583-601.

55. Department of Health, *Social Care Green Paper – Independence, Well-being and Choice*, Department of Health 2005.

56. For example see the Minority Report of the Royal Commission on Long Term Care for the Elderly, *With Respect to Old Age: Long term care – rights and responsibilities*, HMSO 1999.

57. M. Goos and M. Manning, 'McJobs and MacJobs: The Growing Polarisation of Jobs in the UK', in R. Dickens, P. Gregg and J. Wadsworth (eds), *The Labour Market Under New Labour,* Palgrave 2003.

58. D. Coats, *An Agenda for Work*, The Work Foundation 2005.

59. D. Coats, *Who's afraid of labour market flexibility?*, The Work Foundation 2006.

60. B. Kersley et al, *Inside the Workplace: First Findings from the 2004 Workplace Employment Relations Survey*, DTI 2005.

61. OECD, *The OECD Jobs Study: Facts, analysis, strategies*, OECD 1994.

62. In the OECD's index of labour market flexibility, the UK's score has moved from 1.0 to 1.1 under Labour, still way below the OECD average of over 2.0.

63. J. Wadsworth, 'Is the OECD Jobs Strategy behind U.S. and British Employment and Unemployment Success in the 1990s?', in D. Howell (ed), *Fighting Unemployment*, Oxford University Press 2005.

64. D. Coats, *Who's afraid of labour market flexibility?*, The Work Foundation 2006.

65. OECD, *OECD Employment Outlook 2006 – Boosting jobs and incomes*, OECD 2006.

66. J. Denham, *Making Work Work*, Fabian Society 2004.

67. B. Martin, *An American Tale*, Catalyst 2002.

68. W. Streeck, *Social Institutions and Economic Performance: Studies of Industrial Relations in Advanced Capitalist Economies*, Sage 1992; D. Coates, *Models of Capitalism: Growth and Stagnation in the Modern Era*, Polity 2000.

69. S. Broadberry and M. O'Mahoney, *Britain's productivity gap with the United States and Europe: a historical perspective*, National Institute Economic Review 2004.

70. R. Jeary et al, *The future of manufacturing*, Amicus 2006.

71. TUC, *Building a modern labour market*, TUC 2004.

72. Amicus, *Unions and Good Work: Results of an Amicus survey on the quality of people's work experiences*, Amicus 2006.

73. M. Csikszentmihalyi, *Flow: the Psychology of Optimal Experience,* Harper Perennial 1991.

74. Equal Opportunities Commission, *Moving on Up?*, EOC 2006.

75. C. Howarth and P. Kenway, *Why worry any more about the low paid?*, New Policy Institute 2004; S. Sachdev, *Paying the cost: public private partnerships and the public sector workforce,* Catalyst 2004.

76. D. Katungi, E. Neale and A. Barbour, *People in low paid informal work: 'Need not greed'*, Policy Press 2006.

77. R. Taylor, 'The delusions of the British Business Model', *Renewal* Vol 14 No 1, 2006.

78. C. Lloyd and J. Payne, 'On the "Political Economy of Skill": Assessing the Possibilities for a Viable High Skills Project in the United Kingdom', *New Political Economy*, 7, 3, 2002, 367-395.

79. TUC, *Submission to Leitch Review*, TUC 2005.

80. TUC, *2020 Vision for Skills*, TUC 2006.

81. J. Healey and N. Engel, *Learning to Organise*, TUC 2003.

82. J. Hannah and M. Fischer, 'Trade unions, globalization and training: initiatives in Britain and Brazil', *in Global Unions? Theory and Strategies of Organized Labour in the Global Political Economy,* Routledge 2002.

83. TUC, *A bookshelf or bookclub in every workplace*, TUC 2006.

84. ODPM, *Sustainable Communities: Homes For All*, ODPM 2005.

85. B. Thomas and D. Dorling, 'Know your place: inequalities in housing wealth', in S. Regan (ed), *The Great Divide: an analysis of housing inequality*, Shelter 2005.

86. Marc Francis, *Building Hope – The case for more homes now*, Shelter 2005.

87. Kate Barker, *Review of Housing Supply*, HM Treasury 2004.

88. K Cahill, *Who Owns Britain?*, Canongate Books 2002.

89. See Iain Maclean, *Land Value Tax*, Compass Thinkpiece 2006.

90. S. Regan (ed), *The Great Divide: an analysis of housing inequality,* Shelter 2005.

91. See www.iceclt.org/clt/cltfaqs.html#how.

92. Cross-sector Work Group on Community Ownership and Management of Assets, *Communities Taking Control*, ODPM & Home Office 2006.

93. TUC, *Slaying the Red Tape Myths*, TUC 2006.

94. J. Chapman et al, *The Long Game, Demos 2003;* J. Braithwaite, *Markets in Vice, Markets in Virtue*, OUP 2005.

95. A. Slaughter, *A New World Order*, Princeton University Press 2004.

96. F. Road, *Out of Pocket,* Citizens Advice 2006.

97. TUC, *Investment chains,* TUC 2006.

98. Federation of Small Businesses, *What can Small Businesses do for Europe?*, FSB 2006.

99. See for example S. Davis, and D. Pitt-Watson, 'Agenda for a civil economy', in R. Liddle and M. Rodrigues, *Economic reform in Europe – priorities for the next five years,* Policy Network 2004; Also see Which, *Time for a Change*, Which 2005.

100. www.corporate-responsibility.org/.

101. N. Isles, *Life at the Top,* The Work Foundation 2005.

102. M. Sawyer, and K. O'Donnell, *A Future for Public Ownership,* Lawrence & Wishart 1999.

103. R. Taylor, *Sweden's New Social Democratic Model*, Compass 2005.

104. A. Turner, *Just Capital*, Macmillan 2002, p241.

105. P. Robinson, *Ten Key Challenges for CSR 2007 and Beyond*, ippr 2006.

106. HM Treasury, *Long term public finance report*, HMT 2005.

107. J. Hills, *Inequality and the State*, Oxford University Press 2004.

108. N. Pearce et al (eds), *Social Justice – building a fairer Britain,* ippr 2005, p392.

109. L. Bamfield and R. Brooks, *Narrowing the Gap*, Fabian Society 2006.

110. A. Alesina et al, 'Inequality and happiness: are Europeans and Americans different?', *Journal of Public Economics 88*, 2004.

111. R. Wilkinson, *The Impact of Inequality,* Routledge 2005.

112. T. Sefton, 'Give and take: public attitudes to redistribution', in A. Park et al, *British Social Attitudes 22nd Report: Two terms of New Labour: the public's reaction,* Sage 2005.

113. J. Hills, *Inequality and the State*, Oxford University Press 2004.

114. For example, see Iain McLean, *Land Value Tax*, Compass Thinkpiece 2006; or D. Maxwell and A. Vigor (eds), *Time for Land Value Tax?*, ippr 2005.

115. N. Pearce et al (eds), *Social Justice – building a fairer Britain,* ippr 2005, p388, Fig 16.2.

116. W. Paxton et al, 'Foundations for a Progressive Century', in N. Pearce et al (eds), *Social Justice – building a fairer Britain,* ippr 2005, p395.

117. Guardian/ICM poll – David Adam and Patrick Wintour, 'Most Britons willing to pay green taxes to save the environment', *The Guardian,* 22 February 2006.

118. J. Robertson, 'The Future of Money', *Soundings* 31, December 2005.

119. S. Dresner and P. Ekins, *Green taxes and charges: Reducing their impact on low income households,* Joseph Rowntree Foundation 2004.

120. R. Peston, *Brown's Britain,* Short Books 2005, pp274-5.

121. Fabian Society Commission on Taxation, *Paying for Progress*, Fabian Society 2000.

122. R. Patrick and M. Jacobs, *Wealth's Fair Measure*, Fabian Society 2004.

123. Robin Blackburn, *Plugging the gap: How employers can help to fill the pensions deficit*, Catalyst 2005.

124. R. Murphy and J. Christensen, 'The tax avoider's chancellor', *Red Pepper*, August 2006.

125. Ibid.

126. Tax Justice Network, *Tax us if you can,* Tax Justice Network 2005.

127. S. Bond, 'Company Taxation', ch 9 in *IFS Green Budget*, Institute for Fiscal Studies 2006.

128. A. Amin, D. Massey, and N. Thrift, *Decentering the Nation: A radical response to regional inequality*, Catalyst 2003.

129. S. Fothergill and J. Grieve Smith, *Mobilising Britain's Missing Workforce*, Catalyst 2005.

130. J. Sacks, *Public Spending for Public Benefit*, new economics foundation 2004.

131. World Economic Forum, *Global Competitiveness Report 2006-07,* WEF 2006.

132. R. Veenhoven, *Average happiness in 91 nations 1995-2005*, World Database of Happiness, RankReport 2006-1, Internet: worlddatabaseofhappiness.eur.nl.

133. Leitch Review of Skills, *Skills in the UK: the long term challenge – interim report*, HM Treasury 2005.

134. C. Leys, *Market Driven Politics: Neoliberal Democracy and the Public Interest*, Verso 2003.

135. J. Frieden, 'Invested interests: the Politics of National Economic Policies in a World of Global Finance', *International Organization*, Vol. 45, No. 4, 1991, 425-451.

136. D. Clark, *The Labour Movement Case for Europe*, Labour Movement for Europe 2005.

137. R. Barrell and M. Weale, *Designing and Choosing Macroeconomic Frameworks*, National Institute of Economic and Social Research 2003.

138. HM Treasury, *The Stability and Growth Pact: A Discussion Paper,* HM Treasury 2004.

139. Euromemorandum Group, *Democratic policy against the dominance of markets*, 2005 (http://www.memo-europe.uni-bremen.de/downloads/2005_English_Euromemorandum 5.12.05.pdf#search=%22democratic%20policy%20against%20the%20dominance %20of%20markets%22).

140. These proposals are described in D. Clark et al 'A Democratic Left Vision for Europe', *Social Europe*, October 2005.

141. ActionAid International, *Real Aid: an agenda for making aid work*, ActionAid 2005.

142. F. Lawrence, 'Multinationals, not farmers, reap biggest rewards in Britain's share of CAP payouts', *The Guardian*, 8 December 2005.

143. S. Haseler, 'The failure of neo-liberalism: "Social Europe" now defines the continent', *Social Europe* Vol 2 No 1, July 2006.

144. For example, see R. Wade, 'Globalisation isn't Working', *Prospect* July 2006.

145. D. Woodward et al, *Growth isn't Working*, new economics foundation 2006.

146. D. Held, *Global Covenant: The Social Democratic Alternative to the Washington Consensus*, Polity 2004.

147. J. Stiglitz, *Making Globalization Work*, Allen Lane 2006; D. Held, *Global Covenant: The Social Democratic Alternative to the Washington Consensus*, Polity 2004.

148. M. Jacobs et al, *Progressive Globalisation: Towards an International Social Democracy,* Fabian Society 2003.

149. H. Chang, *Kicking Away the Ladder*, Anthem Press 2002.

150. K. Gallagher and L. Zarsky, 'Rethinking Foreign Investment for Development', *post-autistic economics review,* issue no. 37, 28 April 2006, 10-32.

151. R. Wade, *Governing the Market*, Princeton University Press 2003.

152. ICM poll to coincide with the release of S. Burall et al, *Not in our name,* Politicos 2006.

153. J. Stiglitz, *Making Globalisation Work*, Allen Lane 2006, pp176-178.

154. www.gapscampaign.org.

155. A. Pettifor, *Chapter 9/11? Resolving international debt crises – the Jubilee Framework for international insolvency,* new economics foundation 2002.

156. See for example, Christian Aid, *Flagship or Failure? The UK's implementation of the OECD guidelines and approach to corporate accountability,* Christian Aid 2005.

157. D. Eagleton, *Under the influence*, Actionaid International 2005.

158. J. Stiglitz, *Making Globalisation Work*, Allen Lane 2006.

159. See www.adeplhicharter.org.

160. J. Eatwell and L. Taylor, 'The performance of international capital markets', paper prepared for the Ford Foundation project *International Capital Markets and the Future of Economic Policy*, Center for Economic Policy Analysis, New York; and IPPR, London 1998.

161. G. Garrett, 'Global Markets and National Politics: Collision Course or Virtuous Circle?', *International Organisation*, 1998; G. Garrett, 'Capital Mobility, trade and the domestic politics of economic policy', *International Organisation,* 1995.

162. S. Spratt, *A Sterling Solution,* Stamp Out Poverty 2005.

163. For more details see chapter 9 of J. Stiglitz, *Making Globalisation Work*, Allen Lane 2006.

164. Fabian Globalisation Group, *Just World*, Fabian Society and Zed Books 2005.

165. See the Global Commons Institute – www.gci.org.uk.

166. R. Douthwaite and E. O'Siochru, *The Economic Challenge of Sustainability*, Feasta 2006.

167. Feasta, *Curing global crises: Let's treat the disease not the symptoms*, Feasta 2004.

168. R.L. Hirsch, R. Bezdek and R.Wendling, *Peaking of World Oil Production: Impacts, mitigation and risk management,* US Department of Energy, NETL 2005.

About Compass

Compass is the democratic left pressure group whose goal is both to debate and develop the ideas for a more equal and democratic society, then campaign and organise to help ensure they become reality. We organise regular events and conferences that provide real space to discuss policy, we produce thought-provoking pamphlets, and we encourage debate through online discussions on our website. We campaign, take positions and lead the debate on key issues facing the democratic left. We're developing a coherent and strong voice for those that believe in greater equality and democracy as the means to achieve radical social change.

We are:

- An umbrella grouping of the progressive left whose sum is greater than its parts.
- A strategic political voice – unlike thinktanks and single-issue pressure groups Compass can develop a politically coherent position based on the values of equality and democracy.
- An organising force – Compass recognises that ideas need to be organised for, and will seek to recruit, mobilise and encourage to be active a membership across the UK to work in pursuit of greater equality and democracy.
- A pressure group focused on changing Labour – but Compass recognises that energy and ideas can come from outside the party, not least from the 200,000 who have left since 1997.
- The central belief of Compass is that things will only change when people believe they can and must make a difference themselves. In the words of Gandhi, 'Be the change you wish to see in the world'.

Compass
FREEPOST LON15823
London
E9 5BR
t: 020 7463 0633
e: info@compassonline.org.uk
w: www.compassonline.org.uk

Join today and you can help change the world of tomorrow

Please contribute generously. Compass is funded solely by organisations and individuals that support our aim of greater equality and democracy. We rely heavily on individual members for funding. Minimum joining rates are suggested below. To join, simply complete and return this form to Compass, **FREEPOST LON15823, London, E9 5BR**. Paying by Standing Order or Paypal means we have a regular income to count on, consequently we are offering new members a discount for paying their membership in this way. To join by Paypal you will need to go to the Join Us section of the Compass website at www.compassonline.org.uk/join.asp.

☐ Waged (SO / Paypal) – min £27.50   ☐ Waged (Cheque / PO) – min £32.50

☐ Unwaged (SO / Paypal) – min £12.50   ☐ Unwaged (Cheque / PO) – min £17.50

☐ Organisation (i.e. CLP; think-tank; NGO) – min £42.50

Name

Address

Postcode

Telephone

Email

If you're already a Labour member what is your CLP?

Positions held

Standing order instructions

Please pay immediately by standing order to Compass' account, Lloyds TSB, 32 Oxford Street, London, W1A 2LD (a/c 2227769, sort code 30-98-71) the sum of £10 / £25 / £40 / Other £ (please delete as appropriate) and then annually, unless cancelled by me in writing.

Bank / Building Society

Bank Address

Account Name

Account Number   Sort Code

Signature

☐ I'm not eligible to be a member of the Labour Party (i.e. you're a member of another political party in the UK) and I would like to become an Associate Member of Compass (with no voting rights).